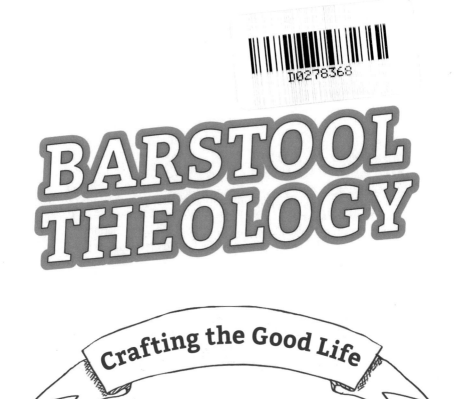

BARSTOOL THEOLOGY

Crafting the Good Life

Trevor Gundlach

OSV

Our Sunday Visitor
Huntington, Indiana

Nihil Obstat
Msgr. Michael Heintz, Ph.D.
Censor Librorum

Our Sunday Visitor Publishing Division
Our Sunday Visitor, Inc.
200 Noll Plaza
Huntington, IN 46750
1-800-348-2440

ISBN: 978-1-68192-357-4 (Inventory No. T2046)
eISBN: 978-1-68192-358-1
LCCN: 2019939960

Cover and interior design: Lindsey Riesen
Cover and interior art: Molly Reynolds

PRINTED IN THE UNITED STATES OF AMERICA

For Dr. Shew,
who taught me how to think

Contents

Introduction

This book is the product of conversations I've had with friends, college students, young adults, and that random dude at the bar, who are all trying to answer the question, "How should Catholic young adults talk about alcohol?"

I began to form my own answer as I lived and worked (as a graduate student who had taken the position of residence hall minister) in the basement of a freshman dorm at the University of Dayton, the last place most people would look for such answers. As I ministered to the four hundred residents, I learned that very few resources existed to help them ask good questions about alcohol. To fill this need, I devoted my entire ministry and graduate studies to research about and instruction regarding how to consume alcohol as a Catholic young adult. I have to admit that a good deal of my research was conducted with a beer in hand! It is good to become one with your research. Practice what you preach, right?

This book includes an eclectic mix of conversations with young adults, lessons learned from personal experience, and theological research. Additionally, I was blessed with the opportunity to develop and teach a class during my graduate studies titled A Theology of Alcohol and Christianity: Learning How to Celebrate. My students unknowingly provided the earliest edits to the content of this book as they candidly expressed interest or uninterest in the lecture material and class discussions.

In short, this book is for young adults, from a young adult. Enjoy!

Stuck Between a Bock and a Hard Place

I like to write down the questions and comments I get when I tell people I study the "theology of alcohol." Here are a few of my favorites:

- Is the wine in the Bible *really* wine, or is it un-fermented grape juice?
- I read a blog once that said people who drink are going to hell. That's true, right?
- Don't Christians believe that alcohol is the "devil's liquid"? My pastor reminded me before I came to college not to fall into the temptation of sin.
- Aren't Catholics hypocrites since they party hard and then go to church the next day?
- Jesus made water into wine and was called a drunkard so ... that means I can drink, right?

Admit it, you probably opened this book with some of the same questions. We all bring to the table (or to the bar) a number of opinions about alcohol. It is even likely that our respective understandings of Christianity differ as much as our opinions on alcohol. We are a diverse crowd, like the people who gather at a party. Therefore, it may be helpful from the beginning to explain what I will and will not address. Let us create a roadmap for our journey ahead.

Let's start by looking to the past. Many people have talked about alcohol throughout the course of history. The topic is always popular because of the effect that the liquid has on our body. Scholars in practically every field of academia have written articles and books to tackle some of the questions that I listed above. Their opinions range from defenses of drunkenness to proclamations of abstinence, from "Carpe diem!" to "You're living in sin!" The average person who reads these articles or hears these sermons is stuck between a bock and a hard place.[1] We ask ourselves, "What is the 'right' thing to do? Is it 'wrong' to drink? What should I do?"

Like most ethical decisions regarding "hot-button issues," it's hard to determine what is "right" and what is "wrong" when we are surrounded by the opposing voices of society, religion, family, and friends.

So where do we go from here?

The goal of this book is to examine moral aspects of alcohol within Christianity without talking about the subject in the way one might expect. I am purposely avoiding the question: "Is it right or wrong to drink alcohol?" Students of philosophy quickly realize that ethical questions such as "Is it right or wrong to do *x*, *y*, or *z*" rarely have a black or white answer. The philosophy textbooks and bestsellers that prescribe such principles teach us that decisions are right if they fit a certain set of criteria, or wrong if they fit another. Does this simplistic approach to life sound familiar?

Instead of falling prey to such an unrealistic view of the world, I invite you into a gray area that exists between the definitive areas of black and white. This gray area, like a barstool, is uncomfortable at first. But, in the small nuances — the slight swivel, the ripped leather, the creaky metal, and the chipped wood — we experience a feeling of familiarity. This seat, like each one of us, has a history.

Viewed from the outside, it might just look like another imperfect stool. But it somehow makes sense within the bar in which it stands.[2]

Let me be clear (for all of you philosophy buffs): I am not making a relativistic claim that there is no such thing as a wrong action. Nor am I saying there is one definite, universal way for people to drink. Rather, I'm inviting you to avoid making a snap judgment. I invite you to step out from the comfort of your opinions and enter into the world. It is here, in the world, where we find that most decisions made on a daily basis exist in this gray area. Each decision is shaded with nuance and detail. Countless variables come into play, and it is up to us to recognize them.

But don't take it from me. Take it from Jesus.

Jesus concluded an abstract teaching to the Pharisees with the explicit command to "go and learn what this means" (Mt 9:13). He knew that sermons, speeches, and lectures were not enough to instill change in his audience; one must go out into the world and learn from experience.

Jesus was one of many teachers who encouraged his followers to live in the gray area and challenge traditions with experience. He did this by asking good questions instead of simply providing answers. Reflect on the following questions that Jesus posed to his followers:

- "Which is easier, to say, 'Your sins are forgiven you,' or to say, 'Rise and walk'?" (Luke 5:23)
- "Why do you see the speck that is in your brother's eye, but do not notice the log that is in your own eye?" (Matthew 7:3)
- "Can the wedding guests mourn as long as the bridegroom is with them?" (Matthew 9:15)
- "For what will it profit a man, if he gains the whole world and forfeits his life?" (Matthew 16:26)

- "Salt is good; but if salt has lost its taste, how shall its saltness be restored?" (Luke 14:34)
- "For which is the greater, one who sits at table, or one who serves?" (Luke 22:27)

Jesus was often misunderstood because his questions seemed like riddles. They didn't have simple "right" or "wrong" answers, which caused confusion and frustration. Listeners were uncomfortable because the answers to the questions drew upon common experiences and were dependent on their own consciences. Why would Jesus trust our individual capacity to make decisions?

Well, he believed, like many teachers believe, that, in the long run, answering questions, rather than listening to answers, can have a deeper influence on the ways we think and act. True personal change happens when we make the decision to change.

Our mindsets and worldviews may change when we reflect upon the right questions (that is, if we are open to them).

These changes can take place in one of two ways: learning from others or learning from our mistakes. Hopefully this book can prevent some of you from making mistakes. Or maybe you have already made some mistakes. In either case, I hope that this book will pose the right questions to help you reflect upon your past actions to help you prepare for future situations.

I will structure this book around five major questions that I've drawn from the experiences of young adults. Each question should help you think about your experience with alcohol:

1. Who drinks with you?
2. What do you drink?
3. When do you drink?

4. Why do you drink?
5. How can you change the way you drink?

I have filled each chapter with theological reflections, comical examples, further questions, helpful analogies, references to ancient philosophy, and stories from my own life. For your convenience, here are the theological reflections that I will propose:

- Who drinks with you? A Theology of Friendship
- What do you drink? A Theology of Art and Craft Beer
- When do you drink? A Theology of the Seasons
- Why do you drink? A Theology of Celebration
- How can you transform your drinking experience? A List of Practical Exercises to Find Fulfillment

As you dive into the sections to follow, I invite you to use this book like a roadmap, not as a philosophical treatise. Highlight roads that you have driven. Dream about future destinations. Go on an adventure! Because there is nothing abstract about the questions we are about to answer. They are simple and straightforward but frequently overlooked. For example, it is not common for us to discuss the concepts of friendship or celebration. We spend time with friends instead of talking about friendship. We party instead of discussing the concept of celebration. But the simple action of stepping back and observing these activities can help spark a change in our mindsets. I hope you learn a great deal about the human experience by looking at these seemingly "obvious" actions in life. Transformation is bound to occur when we stop taking things for granted.

What's on Tap?

A book intended for young adults must inevitably reflect upon the experiences of college students, since college is a time of condensed transformation. It's important to note that I intend any reflections about college to be applicable to all young adults, since college is where many young adults first establish their adult habits. We can learn a lot about young-adult culture by observing a college party.

With that in mind, it is important to ask: How would *you* summarize the current drinking climate on the average college campus?

A national survey conducted by Villanova University revealed that 80 percent of college students choose to drink.[3] This number tells a story: Each student, in one way or another, will come face to face with alcohol during his or her college experience. The fact that alcohol plays such a major role on college campuses is enough of a reason to explore the theological ramifications of alcohol consumption, not to mention the frequent encounters that young adults have beyond college.

Thus, I lead to the thesis statement of this book: We must learn how to make our drinking experiences more fulfilling and less empty. *We must learn how to make our drinking experiences more fulfilling and less empty.*

How will this book, in your hands, help you on your journey? I am glad you asked!

First, you'll notice along the way that I'll frequently return to the theme that "we must learn" how to have a fulfilling drinking experience. This assumes that we don't know how to drink well (not to be taken personally!). It also assumes that drinking in a fulfilling manner does not come naturally. It takes an effort and awareness that we must learn and practice.

Second, we should want our drinking experiences to leave us feeling "more fulfilled" and "less empty." But what brings you fulfillment? I can't answer that question. Only you can. But the questions I'll ask will help you reflect on what or who brings you fulfillment. Fulfillment, in the various ways we experience it, is measured qualitatively rather than quantitatively.[4] Although quantity matters in some fields, such as engineering and finance, we are not here concerned with identifying the "right" or "wrong" number of drinks. Instead, we are concerned with the effect that alcohol has on our souls, which forms the basis of my qualitative measurement.

The fact that I declared a thesis statement means that I will make an argument. I'll try to convince you to think in a new way. As we all know, it is hard to convince people to try new things; therefore, I have dedicated an entire chapter as a rhetorical "nudge" to get you to leave the comfort of your daily grind and go out into the world. Chapter 5 is full of simple, practical actions for daily life (and most of them are legal for people of any age). I'll raise these suggestions throughout the book, marked by sections titled "How." I invite you now to pause reading and flip to the corresponding section in Chapter 5 (on page 148) to explore the "How" below. Take a moment to practice:

How #0: Practice Run: Learn How to Use This Book!
Turn to page 148.
Welcome back.

Disclaimer: Armchair Philosophy and Barstool Theology

"Don't take yourself so damn seriously," advised Father James Martin, S.J., in his commencement speech to the 2014 graduating class of Marquette University.[5] "Don't take yourself so seriously. Laugh at yourself. ... Look, you're about to graduate from one of the best schools in the country. It's easy to get stuck up."

Father Martin's statement triggered a moment of déjà vu: I was transported back to the first day of Philosophy 1001: Foundations in Philosophy. My professor, Dr. Melissa Shew, sat on the table in the front of the room, looking over the faces in the class. Her first words were rehearsed, yet genuine, as they streamed from her mouth and showered our eager ears: "You are about to become philosophers, a title which carries a large responsibility." Then her tone grew more serious: "With that being said, I want you to avoid falling into a common trap. Whatever you do, or whatever you say, do not become an 'armchair philosopher.'"

She paused, letting us soak in the statement. After a moment of silence, she continued her train of thought. "You are probably asking yourselves, 'What is an armchair philosopher?' Well, armchair philosophers live up to the title; they comfortably sit in their fancy armchairs and give answers to the problems of the world. From afar they diagnose each problem and explain how to fix it without getting their hands dirty."

I want to develop the thesis of this book along these same lines by (1) encouraging you not to take yourselves too seriously when talking about alcohol, and (2) offering an alternative, more fulfilling option than what the current culture means by "alcohol consumption."

Sure, it is tempting to stay in the comfort of our armchairs. We see this approach time and again: Many of the theologians who have studied and written about alcohol have never left their comfortable thrones. It is easy for them to condemn or judge the actions of others when they surround themselves with the familiarity of their own thoughts and people who share the same opinions. Many of them take themselves too damn seriously, without taking others seriously enough.

This book, on the other hand, as a theology of alcohol for young adults in the twenty-first century, will not be effective if it follows the method of armchair philosophy. It must take seriously the experiences of young adults. We need a new way to talk about alcohol, one that is rooted in experience and has practical implications. It must also be born from the real lives of young adults. Only then will it be convincing and applicable.

I invite you to get up from your comfortable armchair and join me at the bar. We must become barstool theologians, out in the world. At the bar we won't "take ourselves so damn seriously" because we'll be opening our minds to the opinions of others. The barstool theologian engages in the theology of alcohol with a beer in hand, ready for discussion. Her philosophical dwelling place, no longer an armchair but a bar, is a natural environment for dialogue. Here she can speak her mind, question things critically, and try something new.

Sounds different, right? This new approach, like a barstool itself, may feel a bit uncomfortable at first. But I promise, once you settle in, it will start to feel right.

While we are here, I should mention that your drinks are on me. Each idea I present will be a beer for you to try. What's the catch, you ask? I get to decide what you drink. You may like some beers more than others. Some of the flavors will be new and others will be familiar. You may even want to order the same drink twice if I have chosen well. Maybe, if I am lucky, you will recommend one of the beers to a friend. But let's not get ahead of ourselves.

"Bartender, bring us a round. Let's have a drink."

Chapter One

WITH WHOM DO YOU DRINK?

A THEOLOGY OF FRIENDSHIP

*Morality is what happens between friends. It is not the whole of
the moral life, but there can be no moral life without it.
Friendship stands not just as a single virtue, but also as the
relationship by which people become good.*
PAUL WADELL, *FRIENDSHIP AND THE MORAL LIFE*

Answer the following question: What makes me
who I am?

How many of you answered with "my family," "my
friends," or "my partner"?

Many of you probably answered a different question
than the one I asked. Did you list the names of family,
friends, or coworkers? If so, the question you answered is
"*Who* makes me who I am?" rather than "*What* makes me
who I am?" Such answers reveal an interesting fact about
how we define our identity: We are naturally more likely
to define ourselves based on "who" we know rather than
"what" we do. The source of our identity is more often a
"who" than a "what." In other words, we are defined by
our relationships more than our actions. This is the basis
of a philosophy of friendship.

A Cultural Identity Crisis

Unfortunately, our culture encourages us to define ourselves based on "what" we do rather than "who" our friends are. Think about the experience of a college student: How often do you hear students asking each other the questions "What is your major?" or "What do you want to do when you grow up?" Now, think about the working young adult: How often do you hear the question "What is your role?" or "What do you do for a living?" These questions reflect a popular ideology to which most of us implicitly adhere. It says, "You are defined by what you do, what you study, and what job you have."

In the short term, this ideology can result in many positive things. It can help us achieve high levels of success in the business world, marked by promotions and raises. We may build upon our talents or attain financial stability. The act of "doing" can help us get a house, a white picket fence, and a dog that barks until the neighbors complain.

But in the long run, without relationships, friendships, or community, we will never find fulfillment. Based on this realization, it is important that we break away from the popular ideology of "what" we do and instead consider "who" our friends are.

The first step is to recognize how we define our identity as young adults. We must define ourselves, at a granular level, based on our relationships. The band Family and Friends sings, "I am a collection of the places I've been, the people I've known, my relationships, and my family, my friends." Their music captures the true essence of identity: Every person we meet impacts our lives. That impact, whether it is positive or negative, will stick with us. Over time many of these relationships may grow into a web of relationality, known as a community. As a result, we are no longer defined by one relationship, but by many. Identity grows as community grows.

For many of us, the college years are integral for the development of personal identity. For instance, many of the opinions that we'll hold for the rest of our lives are formed during this period. Our senses of humor will be molded around the jokes and stories that we hear each day. Our use of language and ability to communicate will take shape around the activities in which we participate. As the college years pass, we will learn at an increasing rate how each component of our personal identity, in some way or another, is rooted in the relationships that we make and the conversations that we have.

The same applies to a community made in the workplace. Simple relationships between coworkers can bud into lasting friendships. A cubicle conversation, or a word in passing, can turn into beers after work or basketball on Saturday mornings. A simple invitation to lunch can lead to expressions of vulnerability and trust that help us learn more about ourselves and each other.

We can see, in the examples of college life and the workplace, that community is the foundation for personal identity. Yet we quickly learn that the process of finding a community takes time and energy. Some friendships are made in the first week of college or a new job, then slowly fade throughout the following years. Or random conversations between strangers turn into lifelong friendships. We may refer to this phase in life as "searching for an identity" when, in reality, we are searching for friendship.

Throughout this chapter, I'll encourage you to think about friendship in a new way and reflect upon it at a deeper level.

Why?

Friendship is one of those interesting topics that isn't normally discussed. It evades our reflection because it occurs so naturally between us and others. We tend to take it for granted and, in general, most of us would choose to hang out with friends rather than talk about our friendships. *Most of us would choose to hang out with friends rather than talk about our friendships.* But if we accept that we are defined by our relationships, then it only makes sense to reflect upon these relationships. We can learn a great deal about ourselves (and our identity) when we come face to face with our friendships, the communities we have formed, and the communities that have formed us. Our purpose is clear: We must try to label and understand the communities that give us our identity.

Join me as we answer the question, "With whom do you drink?" We will quickly see how much of an influence, both constructive and destructive, one friend can have on another.

You've Got a Friend in ... Aristotle?

Aristotle's *Nicomachean Ethics* is a text commonly assigned by philosophy professors and is universally accepted as one of the most foundational texts from antiquity. Saint Thomas Aquinas cites it countless times. Catholic ethics draws upon, and elaborates upon, many of the ideas that Aristotle introduced. Among Aristotle's ideas that resonate with Christian thought are his reflections on the human soul, the gift of human reason, and the process of discernment that we must use when we make a moral decision. These are traditionally understood as "philosophical" topics — the type that can put many of us to sleep. Then he explores a topic that isn't traditionally grouped with ethics and philosophy: friendship. According to Aristotle, ethics and friendship are intimately bound together. *Ethics and friendship are intimately bound together.* This connection is worth exploring in detail.

Aristotle proceeds to break down friendship[6] into three groups: friendships of *usefulness, pleasure,* and *virtue.* Understanding each type of friendship will help us reflect upon our own friendships and, as a result, our identity.

Friends of Usefulness

Creating a LinkedIn page is a common practice for most young adults. Career counselors are quick to emphasize the benefits; each "connection" functions as a foot in the door for a potential employer. We can endorse one another and share information through a seemingly infinite network. The possibilities are endless.

But wait, there's more! The entire human race can become a network of potential connections that can be useful for business growth or financial success. Our list of "connections" might start out with middle-school classmates, family members, or that random guy we met in a coffee shop. It then grows to "connections" with those we've never met: a coworker's former coworker, a cousin's current boss, an employee across the world who worked with a neighbor. We can judge our connections based on their ability to introduce us to more people or opportunities. In the end, the goal is success.

I invite you to think about this question: Would you say that you are friends with each "connection" on LinkedIn? Probably not. Does this mean that you should delete your account and boycott the service? No. We all know that these connections are not negative, per se. But it is important to realize that these "connections" do not constitute what most people would define as a strong friendship.

A vice-presidential candidate offers a perfect illustration of this type of mutually beneficial "connection." Presidential candidates will carefully appoint vice-presidential candidates during an election season based on who will represent a pool of voters that the presidential candidates don't reach on their own. The decision is a political move that has repercussions for each party involved. This "connection," a friendship of usefulness, is mutually beneficial.

A similar type of contract, albeit unspoken, is visible on a college campus. Certain friendships are made early in the year that are beneficial for students. Crafty students will seek out the overachievers in a class and will try to gain access to their study guides in the days leading up to an exam. Underage students will befriend the floormate who owns a fake ID, or has an older sibling, to get their hands on a case of beer. We quickly learn who we must know in order to gain access to a particular party. These friends are beneficial as long as they get our names on the list.

Friendships of this kind are good only as long as they are useful, which means they can be discarded just as quickly as they are made. An employee can be fired in an instant. An acquaintance made during the first week of college can be unfriended in later years. For one reason or another, a good number of our friendships remain at this level of usefulness.

Friends of Pleasure

The term "friend with benefits" might come to mind when we see Aristotle use the phrase "friendship of pleasure." Interpreting Aristotle in this modern way, however, would be inaccurate and an oversimplification of what he meant. He used the term "pleasure" to refer to any activity that causes enjoyment. Pleasurable activities, both romantic and platonic, form the basis upon which many of our relationships are made. Most meaningful relationships begin as friendships of pleasure.

Let us compare "pleasure," a synonym for enjoyment in Aristotle's thesaurus, to the philosophy of dating websites. Behind every successful dating website is a complex web of algorithms that determines compatibility based on the hobbies and interests of each member. A "match" is made based on shared activities that are enjoyable for both parties. The first date normally includes one of these common activities. Matched couples will go bowling, hiking, or simply meet over coffee.

People feel more comfortable spending time with a stranger when there is a shared activity. Consider planning a first date or a party: The itinerary normally revolves around an action. The simple acts of getting together for coffee, a meal, or a beer fall under this category. Most actions done in a group have a similar goal: enjoyment. Groups form when multiple people receive enjoyment from the same activity.

These groups can be a powerful source of identity. Students sign up for clubs, intramural sports teams, or service fraternities because they know that the club will plan activities. Coworkers will join volleyball leagues or prayer groups. The club exists to help the members come together.

Often all is well within the group until the members run out of things to do. Problems are prone to arise in a group when the shared activity reaches completion or is removed. Players on a pickup basketball team return to their respective apartments after the final buzzer. Parties are broken up and groups disband when the keg runs dry. In general, friendships of pleasure can easily lapse into confusion in the absence of a shared activity. Friends must start another activity if they want to stay together without things becoming awkward.

One community in particular comes to mind when we talk about shared actions among young adults: the gathering of friends for the sake of drinking (a.k.a., a party). In conversations among young adults on a Friday afternoon, the question "What are we doing tonight?" is the anthem of the weekend. Drinking alcohol is a shared activity around which many students and young adults gather because the convivial effects are conducive to pleasure. The ritual of the weekend begins with purchasing alcohol, continues at a party, and ends when the alcohol runs out.

Yet, the simple goal of pleasure can easily be abused when a deeper goal is absent. Friends become pleasure-seekers, focusing only on the enjoyable effects of the alcohol. They support one another in this quest for pleasure. It is no wonder that this pleasure can quickly turn into drunkenness; drunkenness results from our unquenchable thirst for pleasure. *Drunkenness results from our unquenchable thirst for pleasure.*

One way to deter someone from seeking a certain type of pleasure is by presenting other, more pleasurable experiences. For example, we may avoid drinking to the point of drunkenness if we want to avoid a hangover. We may abstain from overeating because we do not want to feel sick. That said, the desire to enjoy physical health, while it might be successful in deterring some from drunkenness, is not in itself sufficient for everyone — for some, getting drunk becomes the only goal worth striving for.

As noted above, gathering for the sake of a pleasurable activity has limitations. These limitations can be summed up in the thought of social justice advocate and renowned spiritual writer Jean Vanier. Vanier founded L'Arche, a faith-based community in which individuals with mental/physical disabilities live together with individuals without mental/physical disabilities. He contrasts two different groups that may form when people gather: *collaboration* and *communion.*[7]

According to Vanier, *collaboration* means "working together for a common goal." Think about the common goals that are shared at the gatherings you attend. These goals can be constructive, such as working together, learning together, serving at a food pantry, or cheering on a sports team. Or they can be destructive, like a violent mob trying to attack a target. In both cases, Vanier would say that the downside of collaboration lies in the fact that we can gather without "really caring for each other or being bonded together in love."[8] According to his definition, even a constructive gathering can share a set of nondestructive goals that are not rooted in love.

The language that Vanier uses to define collaboration is identical to the language that we have used thus far to define a friendship of pleasure. The relationship is uncanny. With this in mind, we can confidently say that a friendship of pleasure is the result of collaboration. A common goal is shared: the pleasure itself.

We can readily observe the logic of collaboration in our relationships. Gatherings can be as innocent as a crowd at a basketball game or a potluck shared at an apartment. The common goals are entertainment, or laughter and happiness. But we also see parties where binge drinking is encouraged. We hear about riots that break out at the end of sporting events, resulting in injury and property damage. In these cases, the common goal, originally a positive thing, has become destructive. At the end of each collaboration we are left to decide whether the goal is achieved through constructive or destructive means. Collaboration allows for both construction and destruction.

Vanier is keenly aware of the dangers associated with these meetings of pleasure (collaborations). In response, he proposes a second type of gathering. This proposal is not altogether different from the first one. Rather, it is a transformation of what we have defined as "collaboration." This transformation takes and rearranges the elements of collaborations with a greater purpose in mind. Most important, it avoids the potentially destructive results of pleasure.

This second type of gathering is a *community*, drawn from the root word "communion." A community, in its truest sense, is an interconnected and interdependent network of individual communions. Each person shares a particular bond with the others, which, as a result, strengthens and supports the entire group. Vanier explains, "Communion is bonding, caring, and sharing which flows and find its fulfillment in celebration." Friends who enter into a communion care deeply about fulfillment and celebration (Chapter 4). They care more about their friends' searches for fulfillment than their own selfish searches for pleasure. They put their friends' needs before their own needs.

This bit of wisdom from Vanier has set the stage for Aristotle's third type of friendship. Vanier, like Aristotle, knows that each type of gathering can be transformed into something greater. Both realize that humans can move beyond mere usefulness or pleasure into a communion of true love. According to Aristotle, the bond of this communion is not usefulness or pleasure. It is virtue.

Friends of Virtue

On a rainy afternoon in Belfast, Ireland, two religious leaders met for a drink at a local coffee shop. Clad in their respective religious garb, they received questioning glances from onlookers who raised eyebrows and peered over their cups of coffee. For the citizens of Belfast, this was an unusual sight.

That day, Reverend Steve Stockman, a Methodist pastor, and Father Martin Magill, a Catholic priest, shared what would be a life-changing cup of coffee.[9] The two men met, as representatives of their respective traditions, to engage in an important dialogue. The purpose of their dialogue was clear: to address the hatred that was plaguing their city. The cultural atmosphere was as dense as the air outside; deep religious tensions between the Catholic Church and Protestant churches still existed in their country.

Reverend Steve and Father Martin set out to clear the air. They desired communion.

Their journey began with a shared interest in reconciliation and the hopes that it could turn into concrete action. Amazingly, their hopes morphed, took shape, and turned not only into action, but into an entire gathering! That day the idea of an annual festival was formed, the "4 Corners Festival."

The 4 Corners Festival began with the goal of "Bringing Belfast Together." The name of the festival was adopted from a poem written by Reverend Steve, titled "4 Corners of Belfast."[10] It tells the story of a city where households, industries, and religions are separated by invisible borders. Each community claims a corner of the city without a care for their neighbors. Religious divisions from decades past plague daily life.

Division was the stimulus that caused Reverend Steve and Father Martin to act. Their friendship, at the beginning, was based simply on their shared goal. It was, in the words of Vanier, a "collaboration." It wasn't until later, during the creation and implementation of the festival, that their friendship transformed into a "communion." Their shared goal, rooted in the desire for reconciliation and embodied in the festival, transformed as their friendship transformed. Friendship and festival transformed in tandem.

How would Aristotle describe this friendship? We can find an answer in the conclusion of Reverend Steve's poem mentioned earlier. It states, "May we move from *institutional peace* to the *shalom of God*."[11] Friends of usefulness or pleasure would simply be content with "institutional peace," or the absence of anger. They would be fine with an agreement for tolerance. But we know from the story above that Reverend Steve and Father Martin did not stop there. They did not settle for mere neutrality. Instead, they worked toward transformation. They did everything in their power to transform the tensions of Belfast into the "shalom of God."

The story of Reverend Steve and Father Martin is a helpful introduction to virtuous friendships. Their example teaches us two qualities in particular. First, the positive aspects of our friendships of usefulness or pleasure are not discarded once we enter into a virtuous friendship. They are simply transformed. Second, the fruits of our virtuous friendships are not restricted to the two friends alone. They will naturally spread to anyone within reach.

One Virtue to Rule Them All

It is apparent how, in the words of Paul Wadell, theology professor at St. Norbert College, "every friendship is identified by the good which joins the friends."[12] We have seen how friends of usefulness and pleasure are identified by use and pleasure. We have also been introduced to the virtue that helped form the friendship between Reverend Steve and Father Martin. Next, it is important to define what specific virtue (yes, there are *many* virtues!) defined the friendship between Reverend Steve and Father Martin.

Looking back, Aristotle relied on the virtues that were popular in his time — justice, temperance, fortitude, and prudence — to describe the bond shared between two friends.[13] We can see how the virtue of justice was the initial glue between Reverend Steve and Father Martin, based on their interest in the community and the desire to dispel the hatred between religions. But we can sense in the poem a deeper, underlying virtue.

Recall the memorable line from the Lord of the Rings trilogy: "One ring to rule them all." Similarly, the theology of Thomas Aquinas introduces "one virtue to guide them all." The virtue of charity, often translated as love, is the bond that outlasts all other bonds. Saint Paul, in his letter to the Corinthians, explains, "So faith, hope, and love abide, these three; but the greatest of these is love" (1 Cor 13:13). It holds together a friendship in moments when other virtues are abandoned for other goals. It is here that we must part ways with the philosophy of Aristotle and dive deeper into the realm of theology.

The virtue of charity is important because of its source: the Trinity. God is love, and the three Persons within the Trinity are a communion of love. The love between the Father and the Son is the most perfect love that exists, so perfect that it is a Person — the Holy Spirit. This perfect love does not exist only within the Trinity. It plays an important role in our lives and is experienced in our friendships as the virtue of charity. According to Aquinas, "We have [charity] neither by nature, nor as acquired, but as infused by the Holy Spirit, who is the love of the Father and the Son."[14] Therefore, we experience the virtue of charity in our friendships when we participate in the same type of love that is shared in the Trinity.

Our friendships are elevated to friendships of virtue when we open ourselves up to the work of the Holy Spirit. But what does this process look like?

It is much simpler than you'd expect.

The Journey of Friendship

Even after the friendship between Reverend Steve and Father Martin and the 4 Corners Festival received global recognition, they both described the entire movement as a simple, organic process. It started with coffee and continues over coffee. We can apply a popular mantra to their situation: "The journey is more important than the destination." Friendship is not defined by the destination (awards and recognition) but by the journey (coffee and conversation).

It is evident that the transformation of a friendship does not happen quickly. We should not expect to be swept away to a mountaintop to witness a great transfiguration. Instead, we should acknowledge and appreciate each ordinary moment. Our friendships will grow when we pause with the other person and reflect upon the times we allowed the Holy Spirit to push us at each moment during the journey. By growing more attentive to the Holy Spirit, we can better welcome the push in the future. Much like in the example of the festival, the friendship between Reverend Steve and Father Martin was transformed into the shalom of God (a friendship of virtue), which began in the shared desire of institutional peace (the friendships of usefulness and pleasure). They allowed the Holy Spirit to push them through the virtue they shared.

In our friendships, our initial goals (use and pleasure) can also become transformed by the Holy Spirit into a virtuous goal; this goal of virtuous friendship is fulfillment. In fulfillment, the two previous goals are still active, but only as byproducts of fulfillment. Neither of these goals is intrinsically immoral, but they are far from constituting a lasting or fulfilling friendship.

This somewhat abstract theology is easier to understand when we observe our own relationships. Think about a person with whom you share the sentiment "I love you." My wife immediately comes to mind for me. Who is this person in your life? I start by reflecting on the relationship I had with my wife before we vocalized the love (charity) that we shared. We did simple things together, such as ride bikes to the lake, walk around farmers' markets, drink coffee, and thrift-shop. Now we just sit in old, worn chairs, devoting our love to each other and sitting in perfect harmony. Just kidding! We still do all the same things that we did before. But something has changed. These activities have been transformed. We drink coffee and thrift-shop with a shared understanding of each other. We still seek out the goals of use and pleasure, but not as our ultimate end. Our end is fulfillment, or, according to Aquinas, charity; and the more we strive for the goal, the closer we become.

Our new goal is unlike the previous two because it cannot be achieved in its entirety. It is impossible to say,

"Now, at this very moment, I have become virtuous." While we are still citizens of this earth (unlike the type of fulfillment we will encounter when we are united in true charity with the Trinity in heaven), fulfillment is not like the destination of a journey, where friends can eventually arrive. Instead, we learn from the philosophy of Alasdair MacIntyre, renowned professor of philosophy at the University of Notre Dame, that "the good life for man is the life spent in seeking for the good life for man."[15] (Recall, "The journey is more than the destination.") We become virtuous in this life by trying to be virtuous, and we are pushed farther when we allow ourselves to be pushed. *We become virtuous in this life by trying to be virtuous, and we are pushed farther when we allow ourselves to be pushed.* Similarly, we become charitable when we seek charity. Virtue begets virtue. On this virtuous journey, we learn that we must remain attentive to the movement of the Holy Spirit in each small moment in daily life. This is more effective than spending every minute dreaming about some abstract destination. So take the first step in this journey. Remember that trying to be virtuous is a sign of true virtue.

How #1: Plan and Execute a Road Trip with Friends.
Turn to page 148.

A brief word of caution: A common reaction after reading this chapter may be to discard the first two types of friendship and seek only friendships of virtue. I imagine that Aristotle and Aquinas would advise against this. They explain how each type of friendship has some varying degree of goodness. Recall how Aristotle chose to use the word "friend" for all three relationships. He knew that friendships of usefulness and pleasure are good up to a certain point. They can be useful for the progress or success of one or both parties. They even help us experience pleasure. But they are trumped by a friendship of virtue. Especially one that is guided by charity.

Friendships of virtue include elements of the other two friendships, but have a different goal. Virtue transforms the fruits of usefulness or pleasure. It leads to long-term fulfillment and participation in eternal love rather than short-term enjoyment.

The Sacrament of Virtuous Friendship

The journey of virtuous friendship starts with small steps. Let's discuss a theology of these small, seemingly ordinary moments in light of some extraordinary moments. According to the *Baltimore Catechism*, a "sacrament" is traditionally defined as "an outward sign instituted by Christ to give grace."[16] At a minimum, the various Christian churches generally recognize two sacraments. At most, the Catholic Church and the Eastern Orthodox churches propose seven sacraments. Despite the number we believe to be correct, most Christians agree that God's grace is not confined to these moments alone.[17] We must ask, "What ordinary moments in our lives are sacramental?"

Loosely speaking, we could say any communal activity that is rooted in virtue and reflects the grace of God can be defined as "sacramental" (take note here of the lowercase "s").

Catholic sacramental theologians scour the books of Scripture to identify the moments in which Jesus instituted each one of the seven Sacraments. During this search, they often overlook the smaller moments in the life of Jesus when the Holy Spirit bonded the friendships between the apostles. For instance, Jesus formed a group of virtuous friends who came to share in his mission. They walked, ate, drank, and talked with him. These same activities — walking, eating, drinking, and talking — are sacramental when they are transformed within virtuous friendships. These seemingly ordinary experiences are transformed just as our participation in the love of the Trinity transforms friendship. As virtuous friends we receive a number of new "sacraments": the sacrament of friendship, the sacrament of table fellowship, and the sacrament of dialogue.

These sacraments also confer grace to anyone who is lucky enough to participate or be a witness. Think about the impact of this in light of the story of Reverend Steve and Father Martin. It emphasizes an important detail about how we understand friendship: The work between friends is no longer restricted to the secular world of usefulness or pleasure. It is central to the spiritual life! Jesus' community of disciples is the ultimate example of sacramental friendship for all of us to follow. It is also a sacrament that we can share with Jesus, our friend.

Furthermore, the way we think about the sacrament of friendship is unlike the way we think about the other Sacraments. For instance, many Christians put the Sacraments on a pedestal. They emphasize their deep, seemingly unattainable, spiritual significance and forget about the simple physicality that is necessary for each one. We tend to focus on the saving power of Baptism rather than the water that is instrumental in bringing it about. We emphasize the presence of Jesus in the Eucharist and forget about the elements of bread and wine. In each example, we tend to forget that each sacrament requires a "visible sign," some physical item, to accompany the "invisible grace." It is important to ask ourselves, "What would happen if we looked at the Sacraments with a holistic approach, looking at both the 'visible sign' and the 'invisible grace?'"

A sacramental view of life can help us break free from our restricted understanding of theology. Jesus teaches us, through the Sacraments, that spiritual realities are dependent, during our time on earth, on physical realities.

Scripture reminds us that Baptism is dependent upon water. The Eucharist is dependent on bread and wine. Confirmation, Holy Orders, and Anointing of the Sick are dependent upon oil. The spiritual graces are dependent upon the physical symbols to act as vehicles of grace.

A restricted view of the Sacraments can be detrimental to the way we experience the world around us. It is hard to recognize the sacramentality of other experiences when we put the seven (or two) Sacraments on such a high spiritual plane. Many of us are convinced there is no reason to look elsewhere for God's grace if we believe that the Sacraments contain the fullness of grace. "Why bother with these trees when I have the Eucharist?" "Why bother with friends when I have been saved by the water of Baptism?" This mindset has become a limiting factor for many Christians.

It is important, as friends, to encourage one another to recognize the grace of God in both the Sacraments and the sacraments. Friendship is a good place to start.

* * *

We can all agree that the organic development of friendship is more prone to happen around organic substances: food, coffee, and beer. Coffee houses, restaurants, and bars can be seedbeds for virtue. Yet the presence of alcohol is not a requirement for friends of virtue (even though it may be heralded as a helpful "social lubricant"). In the previous types of friendship, alcohol was the object of desire that made a person useful or a conversation enjoyable. Friends of usefulness were kept around as long as the connections they provided us to alcohol or parties were strong. Friends of pleasure drank together, since doing so was enjoyable for everyone involved. Friends of virtue may still do all these things, but only as a byproduct of seeking fulfillment and the virtue of charity.

We have seen how simple conversations about shared ideals can lead to revolutionary movements. Small actions can have massive repercussions, and a few minutes spent discussing the flavors of a particular beer can become a few hours spent mulling over the complexities of all that life has to offer. If we want to experience these fruits of friendship, we must go out into the world and open ourselves up. We must get up from our armchairs and sit at the bar.

But a word of warning: We must be careful! Friendships are risky.

Mirror, Mirror, on the Wall

Society labels free-climbers, cliff-divers, or other extreme sport enthusiasts as risk-takers. Why? These people share one thing in common: They put their physical well-being on the line for a few moments of exhilaration.

I must disagree with this popular definition of "risk" and say that friends of virtue are the real risk-takers. Each time we make a virtuous friend, we take a risk. *Each time we make a virtuous friend, we take a risk.* Friends do not risk their physical well-being. They risk their emotional, psychological, and social well-being.

Being a friend of virtue means opening ourselves to the possibility of being changed by our friend. This process of vulnerability begins by viewing the friend, in the words of Paul Wadell, "like a mirror."[18] We come face to face with ourselves when we look at our friend and, in this moment, we become vulnerable to recognizing our faults.

Think about the last time you looked into a mirror. You either saw what you wanted to see, projecting a set of invented hopes and desires on the reflection. Or you came face to face with reality. You saw things as they really were, imperfections and all.

Friends perform the same function as a mirror: They are mirrors into our deepest self. Sometimes we project a set of personal hopes and desires onto the friend. We expect them to act a certain way or say what we want to hear. Thomas Merton — author, mystic, and Trappist monk — described this situation: "We too avidly seek to find, in our friends and in the things we love, a reflection of our own superior excellence. But we are always disappointed."[19]

On the other hand, if we allow it, our friends can show us who we really are. The friend, a true "other" and not a "reflection-of-me," can change us in unexpected ways. At the same time, true friends also pull us out of our focus on ourselves. When this happens, we are able to see behind all the ideas we hold about them. They are no longer who they "should" be, but who they truly are and who they have always been. Seeing our friend as a unique being, free from our control, opens up the possibility of true, virtuous friendship.

A new friend can influence us in one of two ways: He can help sustain our growth of virtue or he can perpetuate our growth of vice. Virtue begets virtue. Vice begets vice. If we are open to it, a friend of virtue can show us our gifts and also help us discover the areas in which we need to improve. Such a friend, according to Aristotle, is "another self" that helps us uncover our true self, flaws included.[20] Whereas friends of usefulness or enjoyment support our selfish search for success or pleasure, friends of virtue help prune our faults while watering the roots of virtue.

Friends of virtue willingly come face to face with the areas where each of them excels and where each needs to grow. This reality check does not arise out of the selfish desires of either party. It is not a projection or a "reflection-of-me." Rather, our friend holds us to the same level of virtue as she would expect to be held in return. Friends of virtue take seriously the Golden Rule: "Do unto others as you would have them do unto you." They share the same set of criteria: "How can we help each other embody the virtuous life that leads to fulfillment?"

As we have all experienced, the process of self-realization — coming face to face with the areas in our lives that need improvement — tends to be a painful process. Many people avoid self-realization because of this very fact. We prefer comfort over discomfort. We prefer pride to humility. Pride is the comfortable coat that protects us from showing our true skin, and we apply a thick layer each time we project a desire onto another person or onto our very self. Hiding from this deep self is an unfortunate yet familiar tendency.

Humility is the virtue that counteracts the vice of pride. It is the spiritual act of stripping ourselves bare before the reality of each situation. The Latin root of the word humility, *humus*, means "earth." The humble friend is down-to-earth, undergoing a constant barrage of reality-checks. They are always conscious of the way things truly are. This means accepting that you are right when you are right and wrong when you are wrong. Humility means accepting reality, no matter the situation.

In sum, we can say that the friend of virtue earns the label "risk-taker" because of her humility. She risks being shown that she is wrong when she looks into the mirror of her friend. But she knows, deep down, that the risk of being wrong is outweighed by the reward of a virtuous friendship. The growing pains of friendship are nothing compared to the joys of fulfillment.

* * *

Many people think that friends of virtue simply restrict one another from drinking to excess. This is not always the case. It is more common for friends of virtue to encourage one another in fulfilling ways.

Here are a few examples of how friends of virtue can help improve the drinking experiences of one another. We can encourage the consumption of artistic craft beer over domestic beer (Chapter 2). We can allow the conversations to oscillate naturally between surface-level topics and deep discussion. Finally, we can remind one another about the reason why we are celebrating (Chapter 4). The phrase "Whoa, slow down" is replaced with "This craft beer is incredible; try this!" or "I am so glad that we can celebrate your new job!" Friends of virtue hold each other to a higher standard of fulfillment, and their gatherings reflect it. *Friends of virtue hold each other to a higher standard of fulfillment, and their gatherings reflect it.*

How #2: Go on a "Friend-Date" with a "Friend-Crush."
Turn to page 150.

Before moving on, it is important to ask the question, "Who teaches us how to drink?" In the next section we will explore the role that mentors play in the lives of students.

The Tipsy Leading the Tipsy
Many professors reminisce about the days when they would meet students at the local bar to continue the conversations that began in class. Office hours overlapped with happy hour, and students grew in their ability to dialogue about difficult topics in a casual setting.[21] But the sheer act of drinking with an adult taught students more than any of the words that were spoken. They were given the opportunity to observe a master-apprentice relationship.

The system of master-apprentice was the common structure of education in Greco-Roman antiquity. People learned a trade by following in the footsteps of a master. A vast number of trades functioned in this manner, including sculpture, rhetoric, architecture, acting, and philosophy, to name a few. Students followed a particular teacher and aided him in research or writing. During this process, the masters could talk only so much about a topic before the apprentice had to try his own hand at the art. Apprentices learned by acting rather than mere discussion.

The master-apprentice relationship has been in a state of consistent decline since antiquity. Today, for example, only a lucky few students are given the opportunity to collaborate with professors on personal research. These students compete unrelentingly for such positions because they know that the experience is priceless. They are told that an employer is more likely to recruit students with imperfect grades who have practical experience than to hire students with perfect grades and no experience. Within this reality, despite the dwindling presence of the master-apprentice relationship, we can see here how it is still (implicitly) respected in society. The competitive edge that is gained through experience is one reason why the master-apprentice relationship is still sought by employers and students alike.

It is uncommon in our contemporary society, which emphasizes independence and personal strength, to hear about apprenticeships or mentoring opportunities. We are rarely invited to seek out a "master" who can help us in daily decisions. The same applies within the contemporary workplace. "Who teaches us how to manage our time well?" "Who teaches us how to balance our physical health, psychological health, and spiritual health?" And, most important to this book, "Who teaches us how to drink?" *Who teaches us how to drink?*

Very few students are taught how to drink in a fulfilling manner before going to college. For many of us, college is a time of moral exploration where role models of how to drink in a fulfilling way are absent. Many students encourage one another to desert the values of their families as they become their own unit, an "independent" person. Although some parental influence will remain imprinted on each student, reminders to "do the right thing" or "be good" fade into the background. They are replaced by the campus culture as students are left to their own devices.

To illustrate this point, I invite you to follow the journey of a first-year college student, Lucy, from day one. Lucy arrives at college with one specific perspective on alcohol consumption. Her opinion, like many of her peers, has been acquired from the drinking culture of her family. Fortunately for her, her father would have only an occasional beer or glass of wine during large reunions. Alcohol never played a central role in gatherings, so she never thought much of it. It remained in its proper place.

Lucy observes in her classmates a variety of attitudes and opinions about alcohol that range from demonization to abuse. She has heard beer described as a "forbidden fruit" and a "golden calf." Some avoid it at all costs. For others, it serves as the bonding agent in relationships. Regardless, Lucy knows that she is lucky; it is uncommon for students like her to be introduced to alcohol in a healthy manner before college. She knows that she will soon enter into a new community with a drinking culture that is impossible to avoid and unlike anything that she has experienced.

The adults in the picture — parents, professors, counselors, and ministers — try to provide a positive influence in a manner of ways. Some parents try to counter the "problem" of drinking by providing constant ethical reminders along the way. We jokingly label them "helicopter parents." This approach is ineffective for the average young adult.

Another approach elevates faculty or staff to the role of surrogate parents. Adults in these roles can exert a great deal of influence on students. Weekly office hours and conversations over coffee are effective means of guidance. Unfortunately, these relationships are uncommon.

What, then, are we left with?

Lucy is left on her own.

Or … is she?

The first weekend of college finally arrives, and Lucy finds herself crammed into a dorm room. People line the walls, holding red cups full of frothy gold liquid. This is one of her first solo encounters with alcohol. It is a whole new world.

Unconsciously, the innate longing for a master-apprentice system is activated. But she looks around and sees only one option: peers, who range in age from eighteen to twenty-two. Who does she choose? The pickings are slim.

The problem is not that Lucy has nobody to follow. The problem is that she is placed in a situation where the available masters have, at most, three to four years more experience than she has.

Based on a scenario such as this, we should not be surprised when new students like Lucy are swept away by a culture that supports unfulfilling drinking habits. Making the right decision is difficult when her mentor and her peer are one and the same.

So we must ask: How can Lucy make fulfilling ethical decisions when her list of potential role models is filled with the names of her peers? Think about what we have discussed in this chapter so far. Our answer lies before us: virtuous friends.

Virtuous friends encourage fulfilling experiences over empty experiences. They build a community in which each individual is regarded as a unique contributor and, within this type of community, Lucy can lean on, contribute to, and receive from her friends. She knows her own gifts and contributes them. But she also knows her own weaknesses and seeks guidance. In this setting, the titles "friend" and "role model" can coexist in ways that are conducive toward fulfillment.

* * *

I have heard the question posed, "Can virtuous friends drink together?" Of course! But the qualities associated with their particular master differ from those who drink together simply for usefulness or pleasure. The master of virtue desires a *quality* drinking experience with her community rather than the individual pleasure (intoxication) that is gained by the *quantity* of drinks consumed. To this master, a hangover is the physical reminder of an unfulfilling night. Vomiting and stomach discomfort make her grumpy and reclusive. Blacking out limits her ability to recall potentially life-changing conversations. She would rather drink a few delicious beers with a few close friends or share a story, a conversation, or a laugh. She would rather leave fulfilled than empty.

Unfortunately, the goal of most parties is directly contrary to the master described here. People drink for intoxication rather than flavor (Chapter 2). They drink the same thing every night without paying attention to the seasons (Chapter 3). They drink to drink, not to celebrate anything or anyone in particular (Chapter 4). They drink to forget, not to remember.

How #3: Reflect: Which "Masters" Do You Serve?
Turn to page 151.

Entire communities are defined by the qualities that they associate with a master. The members of a community that respect holding one's liquor are prone to consume alcohol on a more frequent basis to increase their tolerance level. Competitive communities respect drinking-game skills and practice their sport of choice. Members of total-abstinence communities are judged by how strongly they are able to define themselves against the campus drinking culture. We can observe how each community is rooted, albeit implicitly, in a common and shared standard of a master.

In the end, friends of virtue are the ones who empower one another to embody the virtues and seek a life of fulfillment. They define themselves according to how the current culture could look if it were to be transformed. Just as Jesus became human to live in the imperfect human community, friends of virtue are actively incarnated within the drinking culture. They do not hide from it; rather, they immerse themselves within it. They transform it from the inside out.

Chapter Two

WHAT DO YOU DRINK?

A THEOLOGY OF ART AND CRAFT BEER

What can I get you?
BARTENDER

*What is art for? This question assumes that there is such a
thing as the purpose of art. This assumption is false.
Art plays and is meant to play an enormous diversity
of roles in human life.*
NICHOLAS WOLTERSTORFF, *ART IN ACTION*

Y ou have just scored a lucky seat at the bar. The score
is tied at the beginning of the second quarter, and
the Green Bay Packers have the ball.

All is well in the world.

You settle into your chair and lean forward to get a
better look at the taps. A difficult decision lies ahead of
you: ordering a drink.

A number of variables are at play. The bar has a hap-
py-hour special, one of the beer labels is attractive, and
your friend recommended something a few days ago. Your
decision just became more complex. The thought crosses
your mind, "Man, am I overwhelmed! The recent growth

in craft beers has made the decision-making process more difficult. There are like thirty beers on tap, not including the bottle list! Sheesh!"

You order a water to buy some time.

With a quiet sigh you take a break from the tap list and look up at the television just in time to see Aaron Rodgers throw up a beautiful pass. Touchdown!

This moment of celebration is interrupted by the man sitting on the stool adjacent to yours. You think to yourself, "Wait, when did he get there?"

He starts off, "First time here, huh? Are you going to order something or just keep staring at that list?"

He chuckles at his own joke.

You release an uncomfortable laugh, shifting your weight on the stool. The man continues, "It's hard to pick when there are so many choices, right? Don't worry … I used to be the same way."

A conversation ensues and lapses into what appears to be a history lesson. You quickly realize that you will miss the second quarter of the Packers game as your neighbor, in his element, begins to tell a story: "Do you want to know how we ended up with this many choices?"

Your body language tells him "No," but he answers back, "Well, I'll tell you anyway."

"The growth and decline of breweries in the United States is staggering! There are 4,144 breweries in the United States.[22] They range in size from macrobreweries to local brewpubs.

"And get this: We have finally surpassed the 4,131 breweries that existed in 1919 … after almost one hundred years!

"Those numbers appear consistent. A few breweries opened. No breweries closed. Right? Well, that's far from the truth!

"Most people don't realize how deep an impact Prohibition has had on the culture of beer in the United States. The number of breweries has doubled in the last four years alone. Doubled! There were only 2,033 breweries in 2011. Isn't that crazy?

"Those born between the years 1990 and 1995 are turning the ripe age of twenty-one during one of the most exciting periods in beer history."

He pauses, scratches his head, and has a "light bulb moment."

"Wait, that includes you! Cheers!"

You barely even have enough time to think, "Man, this guy is crazy," when he continues: "The number hit 407 in 1950 and reached an all-time low of eighty in 1983. Let that sink in. Eighty. Total."

Chuckling, he continues, "It is no wonder older generations have a difficult time choosing between Bud Light and Miller Lite! Domestic beers were the only ones available for purchase. Sad, isn't it?"

He takes his glass, swirls it, takes a long sniff, tastes it, and continues: "But, let me tell you this. The current growth in microbreweries has macrobreweries shaking in their boots. They are losing customers on a daily basis as kids like you have been swept away by the world of craft beer. Just look at beer ads: You'll see this loud and clear!"

As soon as he says this, the game pauses as the local broadcast pans to commercials. He nudges you in the arm, pointing up at the screen, "Look! What a coincidence! They are replaying the 2015 Budweiser Super Bowl commercial."

You catch a few lines as they pass by: "brewed for drinking, not dissecting" and "it's not brewed to be fussed over." You also catch that they are "proudly a macro beer."[23]

The man releases a hearty laugh, sets down his beer, and continues with a question.

"Do you know why macrobreweries don't want their

beers to be 'fussed over'? Think about this: Coors Light wants you to drink their beer when it's ice cold. The mountains on the can even turn blue when it's at optimal temperature, which is 39 degrees."

You have a sudden flashback to the night before in your friend's apartment. You were handed a beer. The mountains were blue. You didn't notice much else. He interrupts your daydream.

"Most people never question these directions. But let me draw your attention to British bar culture. I visited in college and the beer is served cool, not cold, between 45 and 55 degrees. Interesting, right?

"Think about the last can of microbrew you had. A popular trend in microbrewing culture is to label each can or bottle with a 'Best Served At' temperature. Why do the Brits and microbrewers ignore the dream of a frosty mug full of ice-cold beer?"

You sit in silence, trying to appreciate his logic. The game has reached halftime, and you still don't have a drink. It doesn't matter because, with even more passion, your neighbor continues.

"The chemistry doesn't lie! Beverages release less aromatic notes and have a weaker flavor when they are enjoyed below a certain temperature. Also, you feel more of that tingly, bubbly carbonation on your tongue when a drink is colder. Nice, right?

"Warm drinks release more alcohol vapors, which distort the balanced flavor. Have you ever heard of someone who likes a warm beer? Of course not! That's why. The alcohol overpowers any other notes that were previously there."

Your daydream resumes, and you are back in your friend's apartment with the same beer. But an hour has passed. The mountains aren't blue any more — and you notice! The thought crosses your mind: "I mean, I guess this guy isn't crazy after all, right?"

He goes on. "Macrobreweries want you to smell and taste less of their beers, while experiencing a more pronounced tingling sensation. They want you to drink it super cold because they want to cover up how it tastes. Now how does that make you feel?"

He picks up his beer, goes through the same ritual as before, and sets it down. You check your watch and realize a lot of time has passed. But you are on the edge of your seat — proof that you are interested in the conversation that has unfolded. The game resumes as the Packers receive the kickoff. All is well in the world, other than the glaring fact that you still don't have a beer. Your neighbor, once again recognizing your indecisiveness, gives you some options.

"Most people take one of two paths: You can surrender, ignore all the choices, and play it safe with a domestic beer. Or you can sit there, like you are now, overwhelmed by the long list, eventually take a gamble, and pick one randomly. Neither option is wrong; nor is it safe.

"But I'll let you in on a secret. You can take a third route. The road less traveled, if you will. At first, it'll feel like you are wandering, choosing random beers. But over time, and after tasting a gamut of beers, you'll learn to analyze confidently the available choices, with a greater awareness of your personal preferences. You'll start to view the beers like works of art. The act of walking into a bar will become like walking into an art museum. *You'll start to view the beers like works of art. The act of walking into a bar will become like walking into an art museum.* My wife prefers impressionism. I prefer abstract minimalism. But we both appreciate other time periods and styles. It'll depend on the day. Your decisions will alternate between comfort and spontaneity. You'll learn what you prefer, while constantly trying new things. Only then will you be able to make a well-constructed decision. And, in truth, it's more fun that way!"

You let slip a laugh at the absurd nature of his rhetoric. You wouldn't be surprised if in that instant he were replaced by an overly passionate art student. But then you think about it. "Do I think about alcohol as a work of art? Would this change my experience and the decisions that I make while drinking? Maybe I will give it a try."

You return from your reflections to a pint glass full of an orangish brown beer. Your neighbor explains, "I did you the honor; it's an Oktoberfest. Local brewer. Perfect for the weather. So how bout 'dem Packers?"

The Art of the Loincloth

Would Adam and Eve's leaf clothing be considered the first fashion line?

Surely not. It's hard to imagine Eve strutting down the runway at New York Fashion Week.

Why?

Let's think about the origin of clothing. The earliest humans created clothing out of necessity. They used animal skins, felt, and flax to provide protection from the environment. It was based on survival.

Now, think about the role that clothing plays in today's culture. Companies don't generally market their products saying, "Our product will help you cover your body to survive the elements." Rather, they assume that just about everyone has clothing; we have met the minimum criteria for survival. That means manufacturers can focus on styles and trends, highlighting different patterns, fabrics, and colors.

The development of clothing over time reflects an important quality of human nature: We have a track record of turning simple actions, done out of necessity and for the sake of survival, into art. *We have a track record of turning simple actions, done out of necessity and for the sake of survival, into art.* Once the minimal needs of clothing were met, tailors and seamstresses began using dyes and weaving designs into fabrics. Clothing began to serve multiple purposes.

Similarly, the purpose of architecture was originally to protect humans from the weather and the environment. Roofs provided protection from the rain or snow. Gates and walls kept out unwanted animals or neighbors. A quick trip to an art museum or historical site reveals that humans, after meeting these needs, started to experiment in artistic ways. Each structure was still judged according to its usefulness, but an additional component was added. Designs were carved into the clay. Gems were laid into marble. Architecture began to serve multiple purposes.

The story of alcohol follows a similar pattern. The earliest purpose of alcohol (early forms of wine or beer) was to make water safe to drink. The alcohol killed harmful bacteria that caused infection or disease. It was common for early societies to switch from water to early forms of wine or beer (with low alcohol-by-volume) to meet the basic needs of hydration.

This simple benefit signaled an important development in human anthropology. A number of human societies, more than ten thousand years ago, made developments based on their desire for safe water and nutrients. The greatest change, discovered by archaeologists at Simon Fraser University in Canada, was the transition from a "hunter-gatherer" society to an agrarian society. These archaeologists have argued that the availability of potable water, provided by fermented beers and wines, was the major cause of the transition. Daily life in these communities revolved around the harvest, as people cultivated the grains and grapes necessary for the beer and wine that would make their water potable.

As time passed, people began experimenting with different ingredients to develop more artistic beverages. Some of the earliest extant writings from ancient communities are beer recipes and receipts for the sale of alcohol. The job of creating alcohol eventually became the art of brewing. Alcohol began to serve multiple purposes.

Shotgunning Craft Beer

The story of alcohol has gone through many chapters since its birth as a safe way to hydrate. We rarely, if ever, think about alcohol as a means of hydration. Instead, alcohol has become a source of appreciation and inebriation. The purposes vary depending on the gathering.

Consider the following: A student enters a college house party and fights his way to the refrigerator. Inside, he discovers a half-dozen cases of low-quality beer and a stack of plastic cups. On the table sits a bowl of unidentifiable juice. Answer the question: What is the purpose of this gathering?

Now, imagine that same student enters a different apartment. Sitting on the table is a variety pack of craft beer accompanied by an arrangement of differently shaped glasses. The same question is posed: What is the purpose of this gathering?

Both stories pose an important question: Can we determine the purpose of a party based on the quality of alcohol that is consumed?

Bill Mattison, associate professor of theology at the Catholic University of America, attempts to answer this question. In his ethics textbook he commits an entire chapter, "Alcohol and the American College Life," to it. He answers the question by posing two additional questions (recall how Jesus often answered questions with questions) that we must ask ourselves when we drink:

1. What do you drink?
2. What do you do when you drink?[24]

On their own, these two questions allow us to reflect deeply on our drinking experiences. But let us go one step further than Mattison and make a link between his two questions: *How are our actions (what we do when we drink) related to what we are drinking?*

Think about the two examples that I used to introduce this section. The correlation between the alcohol we choose to consume and the actions we choose to commit is powerful. Liquor-store purchases on Friday afternoon might foreshadow the actions of the evening.

Consider one obvious correlation: We consume domestic beers at a faster rate or in larger quantities than craft beer. Why? Domestic beers are brewed at a lower ABV (alcohol by volume) with less potent flavors. Consumers who plan on drinking in excess or in fast intervals will purchase these beers because drinking them is like "throwing back" an intoxicating water. They are known as "easy drinkers."

How #4: Would You Still Drink Alcohol If It Did Not Make You Intoxicated?
Turn to page 152.

On the other hand, few people chug craft beer. Anyone who has had craft beer knows that it is difficult to "throw back" many of them. Qualities that are present in some craft beers, such as a heavier body, more potent flavors, and higher ABV, cause us to slow our rate of consumption. The purpose of drinking craft beer is generally pleasure, whereas the purpose of drinking domestic beer is more often intoxication.

How #5: Host a "Cheaper Beer" Sampling Party.

Turn to page 153.

Each type of beer, domestic and craft, is commonly associated with certain actions. The nature of each product demands a particular style of consumption.[25]

Separation Anxiety

The frequent abuses in our alcohol consumption suggest a disconnect between our consumption habits and what we consume. What causes this discrepancy? Why do we do what we do?

Michael Pollan, renowned author and accredited food scientist, argues that Americans suffer from dietary problems and issues related to consumption because they are distanced from the foods that they consume.[26] The growth and harvesting of crops; the cooking, fermenting, or aging of foods; and the preserving, shipping, and packaging of products are rarely understood by the consumer. Think about your dinner: Can you name where the items came from or the name of the farmer? Probably not. We purchase a frozen meal from the supermarket or a dinner at a restaurant and only see the finished product that is ready for consumption. Our "ready-made" economy encourages us to keep our distance from the fields, workers, or chefs who all had a role in preparing the dish. The process is safely hidden in the shadow of the final product.

The same can be said about beer production. Domestic brewing companies focus their advertisements on the end product more than the brewing process. These companies have contributed to the same problem that Michael Pollan addresses regarding food production: *They have distanced us from the process of creating alcohol.* We have become strangers to the brewing process who accept any beer that is cold, cheap, and in our hands.

The problem lies in the distance between the farm and our table. Pollan argues that it is easier to abuse a substance when we are ignorant of the source of our food and the process of production. He proposes how we are more likely to consume food in a healthy manner, and enjoy that same food, when we are aware of the process and the amount of work that was required to create it. His most popular book, *The Omnivore's Dilemma*, follows the history of an ordinary American meal at each step of production. Readers quickly recognize that they, the average American, influenced by the current food culture, eat with their eyes closed. We know very little about how our food reaches our table.

Another problem stems from Pollan's initial observation: A consumer who is distanced from the process of production will accept whatever is placed before her without exploring other creative possibilities that are available. Americans living in the Prohibition aftermath tend to be settlers; they settle for things, even when there is a better option. Part of this settling is encouraged by the media. Distance creates ignorance, and ignorance allows Americans to consume without reflection. Macrobreweries prefer ignorance because it is profitable.

Reflection, on the other hand, leads to particularity. And particularity drives us, the customers, to more artistic options. Keeping this in mind, we should not settle for the bare minimum when better options are available. We can follow a simple twofold process to avoid "settling for the bare minimum":

1. Learn the *process.*
2. Appreciate the *product.*

Microbreweries like to emphasize the amount of detail

that goes into making one of their beers. Their products are not simply a science experiment or a marketing ploy; they are an attempt to create a work of art. These breweries want people to understand the process that goes into making their art. They want to bridge the gap between farm and bottle.

How #6: Go on a Brewery Tour, Vineyard Tour, or Distillery Tour.
Turn to page 155.

True artists invite us to appreciate both the process and product of their labors. They realize consumers appreciate the product more when they understand the process. The process reveals the product. The product embodies the process.

Thankfully, the veil between process and product is slowly being pulled back. Transparency has become a trend that is beneficial for both consumers and producers. We are finally experiencing a remarriage between the products that we consume and the process of production.

One example of the remarriage between consumer and producer can be found in Pope Francis's encyclical *Laudato Si*. Francis encourages Christians to appreciate the people who grow, gather, and cook their food. His proposition is simple: pray before each meal. "I ask all believers to return to this beautiful and meaningful custom. That moment of blessing, however brief, reminds us of our dependence on God for life; it strengthens our feeling of gratitude for the gifts of creation; it acknowledges those who by their labors provide us with these goods; and it reaffirms our solidarity with those in greatest need."[27]

Take an extra moment before each meal (or a glass of beer) to reflect upon these words:

Bless us, O Lord,
and these thy gifts,
which we are about to receive
from thy bounty,
through Christ, our Lord, Amen.

Oaky Undertones and Hints of Cinnamon

The book *Wine for Dummies* begins with an insightful quote: "Smelling wine is really just a matter of *practice* and *attention*. If you start to pay more attention to smells in your normal activities, you'll get better at smelling wine."[28] The author encourages us to go around the world like a curious child, picking up random objects and smelling them. Our catalogue of smells and tastes will expand if we allow our curiosity to get the best of us. Curiosity leads to knowledge, and knowledge deepens appreciation. This process can be a daily (even hourly!) occurrence.

Our appreciation of an art will grow in two ways:

1. Practicing (consumption); and,
2. Paying attention to the world around us.

The first point, practicing, is self-explanatory. We broaden our understanding of craft beer when we practice and consume different beverages. We appreciate more flavors as we mindfully consume them. Practice makes perfect.

Our second point, paying attention, requires further unpacking. Paying attention means sniffing and tasting the different elements of the natural world that we encounter each day. We must become aware of everything with which we come into contact. Kneel down and smell the flowers or the mulch that surrounds them. Wander around a spice shop and smell the samples. Take your time when you eat and appreciate each bite. Because each one of these small, seemingly insignificant moments can increase our appreciation of craft beer.

The relationship between attention and appreciation forms a cycle. Our curiosity and attention to the world cause us to learn more about art, which increases our appreciation. This appreciation, in turn, fuels our continued drive to be curious and pay more attention. Round and round the cycle goes, and, in no time, we begin to look at beer differently. It is no longer just a product for us to consume. Instead, beer becomes a lens that allows us to see deeper into the natural world.[29] Beer becomes a lens that allows us to see deeper into the natural world.

How #7: Go to an Art Museum: Learn to Respect Abstract Art.
Turn to page 156.

The person who appreciates art is attentive to details, the natural world, and the subtle nuances that can arise within a certain food, beverage, or piece of art. Even the smallest decision to pay attention to the subtleties in a beer can help us pay closer attention to the world around us. That's why it's not uncommon for beer-lovers to love the entire natural world.

The Community of Appreciation

The two processes of practicing and paying attention are rarely conducted in solitude. That's because artistic appreciation, at its core, has the power to form a community and bring people together. *Artistic appreciation, at its core, has the power to form a community and bring people together.*

As we saw in Chapter 1, it is often our friends who are responsible for inviting us into these communities of shared appreciation. The role of a friend is integral to sticking with a craft because, without proper direction, guidance, and companionship, we may quickly get overwhelmed or discouraged by the vast amount of information surrounding a craft. The following story will help illustrate this point.

Mike just bought his first house and is pleased his property includes a spacious backyard. He has always been interested in farming and organic foods and is looking forward to what he can do with the available greenspace. His friends, in recent years, have planted in him a desire to garden. They always feed him the freshest vegetables and herbs when they gather at community potlucks. One tomato, four jalapeños, and countless cucumbers later, Mike has become hooked.

Here starts Mike's gardening adventure.

He begins his journey by calling his friend Mary, who has been gardening for many years. They meet at a coffee shop to plan his future garden. Mary introduces Mike to her favorite websites, blogs, and magazines where she goes for insight. Mike immediately creates a username and registers for a blog about gardening. He engages on blog threads to figure out what strain of tomato would be best suited for the sporadic weather in Ohio. Conversations online lead to further research. He is drawn in by the vast amount of knowledge on the subject.

One morning, Mike decides to take a rest from his research and leaves on a bike ride. On his way home, he spots a mobile farm stand at an intersection. He stops and converses with the worker, who has been farming for many years. Mike receives some tips, buys a cabbage, and rides home.

Thursday night rolls around and Mike finds himself at a potluck with some friends. He runs into Mary, and they chat about her garden and his research. Afterward, Mary introduces Mike to her friend Meaghan. Meaghan hears about Mike's budding interest in gardening and expresses her interest in the social justice issues associated with farming. Meaghan and Mike talk for an hour about urban farming and the collectives of local farmers' markets. He is grateful for the conversation, even though he has never heard of urban farms. It turns out he is otherwise committed during volunteering hours for the urban farms. Meaghan respects that urban farming isn't his passion, and they continue to share ideas at future potlucks.

As time goes on, Mike finally breaks ground, buys the proper seeds from his local store, and starts growing his vegetables and spices. Some plants wither and die while others flourish. Mike thinks to himself, "Heck, I'll be happy if I keep even one alive!" In a move of desperation, he finds the old scraps of paper that hold the tips from the man at the farmers' market and applies them to his garden. Unfortunately, some of them are unhelpful compared to the information gathered from the blog posts. So he takes to the Internet and publishes them to his favorite blog. Others respond, both skeptical and thankful. This simple post marks an important moment for Mike. He is no longer just an observer. He is a contributor.

The harvest passes, and Mike takes a break from his gardening to plan for the next year. He brings the last vegetables from his pantry to another potluck, where he expresses gratitude to Mary and Meaghan for their encouragement.

Halfway through the meal, one of Meaghan's friends interrupts the conversation and exclaims how delicious the tomatoes taste. She notes they are unlike anything she has purchased from the local grocery store. Mary points at Mike and says, "He is responsible for this! You should ask him about gardening."

The newcomer approaches Mike after the meal and expresses interest in starting a garden. She tells him her family has always canned vegetables, and suggests they share information on their respective hobbies. Mike invites the newcomer to coffee, and the community of appreciation grows.

This narrative teaches us that:

- Appreciation forms a community.
- We always have more to learn about an art.
- We are invited to become mentors once we learn about an art.
- Appreciation is contagious: Once we appreciate one thing we often start to appreciate other things.

How #8: Build Your Own Six Pack: Sample and Compare.
Turn to page 157.

The example of gardening can be substituted with any other form of art. For the sake of this book, let us substitute gardening with the art of brewing and the appreciation of craft beer. Many of the situations are transferrable. What we choose to drink can start conversations at bars, liquor stores, campsites, sporting events, and parties. We can search the Internet or engage in blog threads about different beers and brewing companies. Wherever you go, it is natural for beer drinkers to form a community of appreciation around the culture of craft beer.

Celebrate Christmas Every Day
Art and the appreciation of art are not confined to the secular world. Christians, in particular, have an important role to play in these two areas. Considering the artistic nature of brewing that we explored in the previous section, paired with the Christian call to engage with art, it is imperative that we better understand the role of the Christian in a world filled with artists and their arts.

For the following section, let us turn our attention to the

role of an artist. The *Catechism of the Catholic Church* helps us understand this role. It explains how "God enables [humanity] to be intelligent and free in order to complete the work of creation, to perfect its harmony for their own good and that of their neighbors" (CCC 307). The logic behind this statement suggests that creation has not reached completion and that humans have an integral role in bringing about this fulfillment. In other words, humans are invited to create, side by side with God, in order to "complete the work of creation." God is the creator. The true Artist. Humans are cocreators, described by G. K. Chesterton as "truly different from all other creatures; because he [is] a creator as well as a creature."[30] We share God's role as artist and work with God, using the gifts of creation that he has provided.

The relationship of the Creator (God) with the cocreator (human) appears frequently in Holy Scripture. The earliest account appears in the Genesis story, which teaches us that God made man in his "image" and "likeness" (Gn 1:26). Christian mystics have contemplated this phrase for generations and understand the "image" and "likeness" as two distinct yet complementary stages on the spiritual journey. Contrary to popular belief, "image" and "likeness" are not synonymous. They are quite distinct.

First, each human is created in the "image" of God. Each one of us has been gifted with a rational soul, a reflection of the divine Persons. It is a gift that all humans receive at conception. It is automatic and, without it, we would not be human. We become more and more aware of God's presence within our soul and the souls around us when we explore the mystery of the "image." It grounds us in reality and brings us into closer communion with all of existence.

Accepting that we are made in the "image" of God allows us to grow in the "likeness" of God. An intercession from the Liturgy of the Hours captures this point: "Leader: You made man in your image and renewed him in

Christ. Chorus: Mold us into the likeness of your Son."[31] Growth in the "likeness" of God takes place when the "image" is realized and practiced in our journey of virtue. It is a process of self-awareness and self-actualization. Being a process, it does not take place in one moment, nor is it automatic. It takes time and energy. It is part of our journey.

We must ponder the following question: How, in light of this brief theology lesson, do I recognize that I am made in the "image" of God and work toward the "likeness" of God?

We must again turn to the rich tradition of Christian mysticism to answer this question. It is here that we learn from a resounding chorus of saints, theologians, and Christians throughout history. One common thread is woven throughout their writings: the practice of Christian meditation.

Meditation is the most common means of uncovering the "likeness" of God within us. By this, I do not mean the Eastern meditation of our Hindu or Buddhist brothers and sisters. Richard Foster, author of *The Celebration of Discipline*, explains: "Eastern meditation is an attempt to empty the mind; Christian meditation is an attempt to fill the mind." He continues his important distinction: "The detachment from the confusion all around us is in order to have a richer attachment to God. Christian meditation leads us to the inner wholeness necessary to give ourselves to God freely."[32] In other words, we can say that Christians renounce (renunciation) the distractions of the world in order to announce (annunciation) the wholeness that God offers. A balance between the two, emptying and filling, detaching and attaching, renouncing and annunciating, will help us discover the "likeness" that God offers each one of us.

Christian meditation is also effective for growing in the appreciation of art, which in turn helps us discover the "likeness" that God offers. Recall the point from How #7: Art helps us "pay attention to the world around us." It also helps us renew our relationship with the source of what we consume. Recall, as well, from the section "Separation Anxiety": We must "appreciate the product." In both instances, we can see how the mindset of meditation grounds us in reality and forms the basis for appreciation.

But it's mistaken to assume that we will reach our "likeness" by sitting in a comfortable armchair and meditating all day. Growth in the "likeness" of God must also take place in the actions that follow meditation. *Growth in the "likeness" of God must also take place in the actions that follow meditation.* We are called out from our state of meditation (renunciation) to a state of action (annunciation).

During each annunciation moment we "give birth" to the joy of Christ. We pour forth the presence of Jesus — which we received in our meditation — to the entire world. The Society of Mary, commonly referred to as the Marianists, has a unique way of teaching this theological concept. They encourage all Christians to accept the invitation that Gabriel offered to Mary (Lk 1:26–38), to bring Christ into the world on a daily basis. All Christians are called to give birth, like Mary, to Christ in their own unique ways in their respective environments. Each Christian is called, through individual "Annunciation" moments, to recognize the "image" of God within us and, after recognizing it, to give birth to it. Creating art is a beautiful example of giving birth to Christ, while appreciating the art of others is a way of recognizing the many birthing moments that happen each day.

How #9: Reflect on the Bread and Wine of the Eucharist.
Turn to page 159.

The theology of daily Annunciation moments can and should be applied to the countless forms of artistic creation. The art of brewing, understood under these circumstances, can be viewed as a form of incarnation. It is a birth of Christian "likeness" that can be shared and appreciated in a community. Maybe the brewers at DuClaw Brewing Company were onto something when they named their peanut butter porter "Sweet Baby Jesus!"[33]

* * *

We have learned how the artistic quality of a product (or lack thereof) has a strong correlation with the amount of fulfillment we glean from consuming that product. Fulfillment is tied to art and the appreciation thereof. Emptiness results from a disconnect between the consumer and the product, the human and the artist. (And, ultimately, emptiness results from a disconnect between the human and the Artist of all Artists, God.) All these elements are at play when we choose to consume alcohol.

This chapter proposes that each of us is invited to enter into a community of appreciation wherein variation is preferred over uniformity. In this community, we'll become aware of both the process and the product of a craft. Both are important, and the exploration of each can aid us in becoming more involved in our community of appreciation. We'll be encouraged to stop taking the process for granted as we appreciate the product.

We are now aware, if we were not already, that what we drink is strongly correlated to what we do when we drink. In the next section, we'll talk about the occasions in which we choose to drink. We will see that this choice has a strong influence on what we drink and who drinks with us.

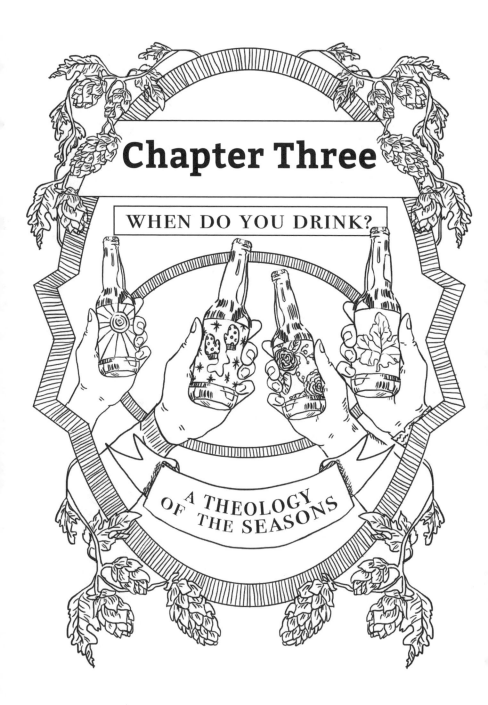

Chapter Three

WHEN DO YOU DRINK?

A THEOLOGY OF THE SEASONS

*For everything there is a season: A time to be born,
and a time to die; a time to weep, and a time to laugh; a time
to mourn, and a time to dance.*

ECCLESIASTES 3:1–4

To say that my mom likes to decorate is an understatement. It sometimes felt like she invented her own seasons during my childhood to create more opportunities to decorate our home.

There were the usual holidays: Christmas, Easter, Independence Day, Halloween, etc. Then there were the unusual holidays: bee season (early spring), beach season (midsummer), back-to-school season (early fall), autumn foliage (midfall), and snowmen season (not to be confused with Advent or Christmas). Each bookshelf, coffee table, and bed stand was adorned with small trinkets or stuffed toys from the local convenience store that fit the theme. No matter the season, whether it was invented or adopted, Mom's decorations would never disappoint.

My mother's passion for decorating reveals an important part of our human nature: It is natural for us to organize life into categorical periods of time. To put it another way, we can say that humans are seasonal beings.

Think back to your childhood. You were taught at an early age to understand the order of the months, the days of the year, and the hands of a clock. These names and numbers are symbolic, much like the plush toys and plastic trinkets that adorned my childhood home. Each time we use them in conversation, we are reminded that humans need symbols of change to discuss time. They remind us of the current season that we are experiencing and help us anticipate the coming seasons. Each symbol is an important human invention that helps us communicate with others and plan for the future. It is no wonder that "the weather" is such a common topic of conversation; it is one of the oldest and most universal symbol sets.

As we grow older, we start to recognize that each season is tied back to one of two universal seasons: life or death. *Each season is tied back to one of two universal seasons: life or death.* These two seasons govern our existence. All other seasons are simply microcosms or derivatives of these two universal seasons. We may derive and categorize our seasons according to our respective geographic location, culture, religion, or family. We may even interpret the seasons relative to the social or political environment in which we reside. But regardless of these variables, the two seasons remain the same. All of existence can be tied back, in some manner, to life or death.

This lays the foundation for the purpose of this chapter: to learn from my mom and adopt a seasonal way of looking at life.

The chapter ahead is organized like a list of "character bios" in a playbill: I will introduce the protagonists and antagonists who will create a narrative in which you can place yourself. These characters are better defined as "archetypes," extreme caricatures that embody the fundamental characteristics of the name that is attributed to them. I invite you to use these archetypes not as real people, but as extreme poles from which we can orient and define ourselves. In most cases they are purposely exaggerated and hyperbolic to help make a point.

We will meet the snowbird and the seasonal person and learn how they experience beauty in the world. Do they see only obvious beauty, or are they able to see the "dramatic beauty" that lies behind the obvious? Can they appreciate the bitter moments in life? Or do they constantly seek pleasure? These questions will help provide a roadmap for the narrative that is about to unfold. Before we meet them, however, let's reflect on beer and its relation to the seasons.

Luckily for us, the seasons also play an important role in the story of beer! The term "the seasons of beer" will help us grasp the seasons of life and death. Each beer that we share, like the plush decorations at my mom's house, can act as a symbol of time and the seasons. They remind us of the seasons of death and life, suffering and joy, emptiness and fulfillment.

The Seasons of Beer

The friendship between Hunter and Sean began at a bar. Propped up on bar stools, beer in hand, they discovered a mutual appreciation for Frisbee and craft beer. After some texting, they decided to combine their mutual interests and meet at the local beach. The plan was to soak up the beautiful summer weather by sharing delicious craft beers and tossing a Frisbee, so they stopped at a liquor store on their bike ride to the beach.

Sean passed a cooler and saw a beer that had been recommended to him a few months prior by another friend. He snatched it up and didn't think to look closely at the label.

They arrived at the beach and slipped off their sandals.

A friendly game of Frisbee ensued. Ten minutes passed, and Sean felt parched. He cracked open his cool drink, took a large swig, and almost spat it out. The beer was rich and dark; it was a porter. He could barely finish half the can before giving the rest to Hunter. A sad thing happened that day: Sean couldn't finish his beer.

Sean decided to try the same beer many months later, on a cold day, to test whether the problem was the weather or the beer. Here are his findings: It was delicious! His friend was right. He had recommended this beer in the winter months when it would have been appropriate and quite delicious. From that moment forward, Sean became very attentive to the type of beer he purchased. He didn't want to make the same mistake. More important, he wanted to avoid wasting any more delicious beer.

This small revelation sparked an interest. The question "When do I drink a certain style of beer?" became important after the beach mishap. He eagerly began to research what styles of beer are most appropriate for different times of the year. He uncovered a gold mine of information on the subject! Sean came to realize that drinking beer, like the rest of our lives, is seasonal.

Based on the story of Sean and Hunter it seems natural to solidify the term "the seasons of beer" in our common speech.

How #10: Learn the Seasons of Beer.
Turn to page 160.

The overarching story of the seasons of beer, like any good story, has two main characters. Both archetypes, the antagonist and the protagonist, contribute to the way the world views beer. Let us review each character and see where we stand.

Antagonist: The Snowbird

The snowbird is the true opponent of the seasons. Traditionally, snowbirds are people who own one house in the Midwest for the warmer months and a second house in the temperate South for the colder months. Biannual moves help them avoid both the bone-chilling cold of winter and the sweltering heat of summer. These people embrace a "snowbird mindset" that says "always seek a consistently comfortable life."

The "snowbird mindset" is not confined to affluent retired folks. It is active in any context where constant comfort is preferred over temporary discomforts. Now, one could hear this statement and conclude, "Okay, time to seek out discomfort!" Let me be clear: I am not saying that we should all become masochists who seek out discomfort. Rather, we must realize that often a greater, more lasting sense of comfort can be found on the other side of momentary discomfort. *Often a greater, more lasting sense of comfort can be found on the other side of momentary discomfort.* Fulfillment can be found on the other side of pain. Unfortunately, the snowbird does not stick around long enough to see that small, natural moments of discomfort can lead to lasting happiness. They opt for constant, unchanging comfort instead.

Let us look at a few examples of the snowbird mindset in the modern world. First, the snowbird mindset has infiltrated high school administration offices. The idea of "teaching to the test" is a growing trend that reflects an illusion of "comfort." Schools are removing courses from the curriculum that form the whole person (physical education, art, theater, and other liberal arts) and are replacing them with subjects that are emphasized on state-issued standardized tests. The school chooses to avoid the difficulties and discomforts of these "qualitative" classes and to focus instead on "quantitative" subjects. Science and math have become overemphasized in particular as art and physical education are discarded. As a result, the students who attend these institutions are forced to become intellectual snowbirds. Administrators make this transition in an effort to prepare students for one single thing: scoring well on a standardized test.

Many teachers and philosophers have criticized this method. They argue that such schools sacrifice the holistic health of students for the sake of one thing: average test scores compared to the scores of other schools. The unique gifts of students are deemed secondary in importance to standardized test scores.

Yet, studies[34] show that schools that cut these courses and "teach to the test" score significantly lower than schools that allow students to "waste their time" in art and gym. Philosophers pose the important question: Why do students score better when they spend less time focused on one subject and more time developing a holistic intellect?

Let us explore another example before answering this question. College students are also conditioned to become intellectual snowbirds. Professors often hear the question, "What is the point of taking psychology if I am a mechanical engineer?" Science students complain about being required to take classes in theology and philosophy, and theology students complain about being required to take an introductory level biology class. Anything other than the classes that are needed for their degree are considered a waste of time and money. We have been conditioned to believe that wholeness and well-roundedness are less important than specialization.

Students take this mindset to heart and start to think that they must cut out anything in their week that does not contribute to getting the good grades required for a standardized test score or a job. "I can't eat! I have to study for the MCAT!" "Sleep? I don't have time. I have to be more competitive for future jobs." These students will grow up and likely cut from their lives anything that does not contribute to making money or gaining prestige. The American work ethic, along with a number of societal pressures, is partly responsible for making students intellectual snowbirds.

Finally, the snowbird mindset also has a strong influence on the beer culture. Many people drink as if there is only one season of the year: watered-down domestic-beer season. For the sake of this section just replace a "Cold One" with the respective cheap beer of your choice. Is it cold out? Have a Cold One. Is it hot out? Have a Cold One. Did you just pass a difficult course? Have a Cold One. Was work tough today? Have a Cold One. Is it fall, spring, summer, or winter? It doesn't matter: Have a Cold One!

Why do people prefer to be snowbirds? Well, for one, it is comfortable. The goal, as we previously discussed, is to seek pleasure and avoid discomfort. The snowbird thinks, "Well, my armchair is comfortable, so why should I leave it?" Second, it is easier. The snowbird is given the option to view life as black and white. She thinks, "If my actions either lead to comfort or discomfort, then why should I ever endure discomfort?" Third, it is familiar. The snowbird avoids the entropy that is accompanied by spontaneity and opts for what he knows. He lives by the mantra, "Why should I try something new when I know what I like?"

All three of the examples discussed — the high school curriculum, the college student, and the beer culture — reflect how the snowbird mindset is responsible for the disappearance of the seasons in contemporary culture. Keep this archetype and the reasons for its existence in mind as we explore the snowbird's nemesis: the Seasonal Person.

Protagonist: The Seasonal Person

Three things come to mind when I think of Wisconsin: cheese, beer, and snow. All three of these things are memorable parts of my upbringing, and we Wisconsinites have all three in excess. But, for the time being, let me focus on the third category: snow.

Midwestern snows are memorable to those who have had the pleasure (if you want to call it that) of experiencing them. But not everyone has positive views of snow. It can be a nuisance for the productive American snowbird. Snow banks accumulate around cars, making them inaccessible. Black ice makes the ground dangerously slick. Lake-effect winds chill to the bone. All these side effects slow us down and cause discomfort. We can hear complaints filling the cold air as students walk to class in below-zero temperatures and businesses salt their walkways. The snowbird's mind is consumed by pain in its search for comfort.

The seasonal person, our protagonist, views the snow in a different light. She accepts every aspect of the snow and even appreciates it. Fresh white powder falls like a plush blanket that tucks itself into the crevasses of the earth's floor. The natural process of death that was observed in autumn is covered and hidden until spring when the world will awaken. Trees are covered in glistening white tinsel. Ice forms and gathers from the gutters. The seasonal person risks hypothermia to hike, ski, or simply gaze at the changes that the world undergoes. Each painful element of winter is accepted as natural and eventually embraced. Although the same painful chill is experienced by both the snowbird and the seasonal person, for the latter it is transformed and put in the context of beauty.

The seasonal person can appreciate both the challenging and comfortable moments in life. She believes that the universal seasons of life and death are each important for growth and that the seasons may offer inconsistency. They may even end in pain. But she has also had a taste of the beauty that is present and available once you stick through the hard times. Something about the holistic approach (seasonal) is more attractive and more fulfilling to her than the narrow method (snowbird).

So, what is it that keeps some of us from becoming snowbirds? What is it (other than money) that keeps the vast population of Wisconsin from escaping south every winter? Let us find out. Then let us apply it to beer!

The Beauty of Risk

The seasonal person embodies one strength in particular that sets her apart from the snowbird: vulnerability to risk. Consider each word.

Vulnerability is a state of preparation that assumes, but does not require, future action. It is a mental and spiritual attitude. Opening ourselves up, the act of becoming vulnerable, is a necessary precursor to risk.

Risk, on the other hand, is the actual exposure to change. It is acting on the vulnerability and the openness that we have fostered. Risk "puts us out there." It is the force that pulls us up from the comfort of our armchairs and leads us out into the world. It is the principle that helps us form virtuous friendships and communities of appreciation, both of which may change us.

Most importantly, risk makes reward possible, and it is necessary for finding fulfillment in certain areas of our lives. For the seasonal person, the reward of risking the seasons is the fulfillment that is found in beauty and the joy that comes from experiencing it. Therefore, beauty and the seasons are inextricably tied together.[35]

The beauty of risk can be experienced in two elements of each season: the naturally enjoyable elements, the things that we might normally refer to as "beautiful"; and also the challenging or painful elements, what we often hear referred to in words that are not appropriate for this book. Both are important for understanding the beauty of risk.

First, the beauty of risk is found in the naturally enjoyable elements. We shall call this "obvious beauty." For example, icicles and snow are beautiful. Flowers are beautiful. The colors of changing leaves are beautiful. These elements are easily taken at face value, and both the snowbird and the seasonal person can experience this beauty.

The second type of beauty is made visible only when we stick through pain and suffering and find beauty in the midst of it. It rests on the idea that momentary suffering can be transformed into something beautiful. Pope Francis, referring to marriage, defines this as "dramatic beauty."[36] This beauty is not obvious, and it requires a trained eye. Viewed through the lens of dramatic beauty, "each crisis becomes an apprenticeship in growing closer together or learning a little more about what it means to be married."[37] Applied to every Christian, married or single, we can say that moments of suffering reveal a beauty that would otherwise remain hidden.

The gospel message teaches us that we will find our ultimate fulfillment and wholeness in a balance between obvious beauty and dramatic beauty. Beauty might be obvious, or we might have to undergo pain and the transformation of pain to finally experience beauty and joy. *We might have to undergo pain and the transformation of pain to finally experience beauty and joy.* With this in mind, we can begin to understand how the snowbird fails to experience the wholeness that life has to offer. She refuses to experience dramatic beauty and chases obvious beauty. In her desire for comfort, she is left behind, and she misses out on dramatic beauty while the seasonal person plunges forward into the unknown.

I have introduced the two elements of beauty to put them in the context of each other. In the following sections, we will look with greater depth at each element — the naturally enjoyable and the naturally painful — to understand how the snowbird experiences only half the joy that would be available to her if she were to embrace a seasonal mindset. We will see that, although she experiences obvious beauty, she misses out on the most beautiful element of each season — namely, that which results from the transformation of suffering.

The Curious and the Obvious

Obvious beauty, despite its name, has become less and less obvious to the casual viewer. It is even common for people to ignore the beauty that the seasons produce. Jesus saw this in the people to whom he preached when he observed that "this people's heart has grown dull, and their ears are heavy of hearing, and their eyes they have closed" (Mt 13:15). The words of Christ extend to people of every generation. All of us suffer, to some extent, from this dullness.

Dullness can cause emptiness and lead us away from fulfillment. In response to this problem, the seasonal person is constantly challenged to find ways to awaken the senses and discover beauty. She relies on one instinct to recognize and receive the gift of creation: curiosity.

We experience the world primarily with our senses. During our initial encounter with something, it either feels good or it doesn't. The instinct that makes us seek out more of the positive "feel-good" experiences is curiosity. Curiosity is the natural sense of longing that we were each given at birth. It allows us and gives us a reason to be vulnerable. On a physical level, it is the creative influence that propels us to act on our appetites (food, drink, and sex). On a spiritual plane, it is the reason we seek out fulfilling experiences. Curiosity holds an important position in this chapter because it is the first step in the process of embracing a seasonal philosophy. Even the snowbird can become curious! So it is important that we start here.

Curiosity is a good starting point for the snowbird, although it has its limits. Unlike the seasonal person's vulnerability to risk, a mindset of curiosity allows the snowbird to stay within the realm of comfort. When we act in this realm, even upon the smallest amount of curiosity, we can help our senses remain acute and avoid stagnancy. The dullness of our senses can be awakened. Compare our understanding of curiosity that has been developed thus far to the definition of insanity that is famously attributed to Albert Einstein: "Insanity is doing the same thing over and over again and expecting different results." Instead, we can say that "curiosity is doing different things over and over again and expecting different results." Curiosity leads us, within a comfortable setting, to try new things.

One of the easiest ways for us to reawaken our dull senses and exercise curiosity is by exploring the different craft beers and breweries that continue to pop up in our cities. You will end up using all your senses to some extent when you enjoy a beer with friends. *You will end up using all your senses to some extent when you enjoy a beer with friends.* Below are a number of new ways that we can use our senses to experience beer. The overall sense experience associated with drinking beer has something to offer everyone:

- **Hear:** This sense is probably the most underrated when it comes to the consumption of beer because it is not obvious. But think about it: Many of the sounds associated with beer are nostalgic. For instance, the sounds of a bottle being popped, a can being cracked, or a tap being poured all instill a sense of excitement for the other senses that will follow. The consumption of beer often leads to conversation or is accompanied by the playing of music. Or college students use the droning bass of a party as a beacon that they can follow to find beer and fellowship. A toast is marked by words of celebration or commemoration followed by the clank of one bottle against another. Then at the end of the night, we hear an eerily symbolic clanking of empty bottles as the recycling bin is filled.

- **See:** A liquor store or beer aisle can be likened to an art gallery. The symmetry and presentation of any number of beers can be a pleasurable sight. The late professor of "Wines of the World" at the University of Dayton encouraged his students to pick a label that looks nice if they are overwhelmed by the number of choices or are unsure of what type of wine they want to drink. He found, in most cases, that the quality of a label is correlative with the quality of the beverage contained within. Along a similar vein, some breweries will employ local artists to design their packaging. Looking at the labels on bottles can teach us that the consumption of beer is not simply a consumption of flavor but an appreciation of the visual arts.

- **Touch:** I have seen a cold beer used as an ice pack to tend to a fresh bruise or a sweaty forehead. As previously mentioned, the cool temperature of a summer beer is refreshing on a warm day, however you use it. The carbonation has a bubbly effect on mouthfeel as the liquid dances and pops on your tongue. Most beers have a warming effect on the body of the consumer: Your cheeks may become rosy and you may experience the phenomenon known as a "beer-coat." You feel warm even though your body remains at a consistent temperature. Some beers drunk during the colder seasons are called "winter-warmers" for this very reason.

- **Smell:** Try breathing in through your nose as you sample a beer. Your olfactory glands, which are the strongest flavor receptors in your body, are located in the back of your nose. By breathing in, you open up the gateway from your mouth to your nose and allow the flavor to travel skyward. The flavor is magnified. This process of tasting is described by whiskey connoisseurs as an introduction between two people. The first sniff is a simple "Hello." The second is a "It is nice to meet you." Then you truly get to know the other as you sample the drink.

- **Taste:** A good amount of experimentation is underway in the world of brewing. Breweries are making sour beers by allowing uncontrolled yeast strains to enter during the process of fermentation. Beers are imbued with peppercorn or tea to add an element of spice. The possibilities are endless! The full potential of your taste buds is also exercised each time you pair a beer with food. Many restaurants provide a complimentary bowl of salty food such as peanuts or chips to pair with your drink. The lucky taster finds a perfect flavor combination between a beer and a food that results in succulence, known in the culinary world as "umami."

Our assessment of the sensations associated with beer would be incomplete if we left out the effects of intoxication. Each of the senses noted above is initially magnified by the intoxication that results from drinking beer. Christian spiritual writers have drawn upon the symbolism of intoxication when they use the phrase "sober intoxication of the Spirit." Just as the Spirit magnifies our spiritual receptivity, alcohol can magnify our sensual and physical receptivity. It becomes easier for us to embrace the world (and our friends!) when our receptivity is increased.

But consumers must be careful not to magnify too far. Imagine that you are looking into a microscope: The image initially becomes sharper as you magnify it. Images and colors begin to pop! But as you continue to magnify, you will eventually reach a point when the image grows fuzzy. You turn the dial on the microscope too far and the colors begin to blend. They turn brown, and then, eventually, black.

It is common knowledge that if we continue to drink past the initial magnification, we will eventually hit a point where the senses become dulled rather than further magnified.[38] Philosophers warn against this stage of drunkenness since it is associated with a loss of control or ability to perceive beauty. The prophet Muhammad warned his followers in the Qur'an (An-Nisa 4:43) to avoid extreme drunkenness because they would be unable to focus in prayer. In a similar way, Paul warned Christians to avoid drunkenness because they might be unprepared for the second coming of Jesus or to inherit the kingdom of God (1 Cor 5). In each spiritual practice we hear a similar message: Don't let your drinking dull your senses further than they already are. This message is especially important in the climate of our current day.

On a more practical note, a drunken person may miss the small encounters with God: a conversation with friends, the sensation of a beer, or the beauty of the natural world. We can summarize that it becomes increasingly difficult to embody the common teaching of Saint Ignatius of Loyola regarding "finding God in all things" when we fail to sense anything.

The beer drinker is in a good position to untether his curiosity and engage his senses. He can use all his senses to enjoy the beer before him and is reminded to appreciate the natural world each time he takes a sniff or a sip. There is obvious beauty in a glass of beer, and our curiosity can help us see it.

* * *

Despite the natural pleasures of a beer, we know, as Jesus explains, that it is not sufficient to simply "see with our eyes and hear with our ears." Although the senses are a good starting point to experience beauty, Christians must "understand with [the] heart" (Mt 13:15). In the words of Scripture, we must incline the "ear of our heart" (Prv 4:20) and see with the "eyes of [our] hearts" (Eph 1:18). It is only through these spiritual senses that we encounter the fullness of beauty that is given as a gift from God.

So far, we have discussed only the obvious examples of beauty that are found in the seasons. The enjoyable qualities of beer, the things that are "right in front of our eyes," have been observed. This obvious type of beauty, as I have mentioned, is what immediately comes to mind when people discuss "beautiful things." But Jesus is calling us to experience something greater than what is right in front of our eyes. He wants us to see a new type of beauty.

We must now turn our attention to the second category of beauty that is experienced by the seasonal person. This second category, which has been labeled "dramatic beauty," results from a transformation of the naturally painful elements. We rarely hear it discussed because it is often overlooked or avoided. It sits in the shadow of the obviously beautiful elements. It is only the seasonal person who can see past the momentary discomfort that is associated with "dramatic beauty." She discovers the beauty that lies hidden beneath the pain.

Each Christian is invited to experience a whole new level of existence that is only visible to those who can see the "dramatic beauty" in life. Jesus invites us to walk this journey, side by side with his mother, Mary; with her we will experience intense suffering at the foot of the cross and intense joy at the sight of the empty tomb. The two, suffering and joy, are experienced together. We begin to see all of life in a new light when we start to see the "dramatic beauty" beneath and within the obvious beauty.

The "Dramatic Beauty" of Beer

Complex theological ideas such as "dramatic beauty" become easier to understand if we can relate them to our experience of beer. Let's talk beer one more time before we dive deeper into a philosophy of the seasons.

Most people enjoy beer at face value: Does it taste good or not? This mindset is fine for the snowbird but is inadequate for the community that is open to transformation. With a little bit of guidance, we can see how the most important step of production — fermentation — and one of the primary ingredients of beer — hops — are both symbols of great transformation and "dramatic beauty." These two elements may help the consumer experience the second type of beauty, "dramatic beauty," in the seasons of beer. They may even help the secular reader understand the importance of "dramatic beauty" in daily life. As we will see, fermentation and hops are like the Resurrection moment after the crucifixion: They can bring great joy to us in unexpected ways!

Fermentation: Fermentation occurs everywhere. Natural sugars found in fruits, vegetables, and grains react with natural yeast cells to create two products: alcohol and carbon dioxide. You might witness this biological process if you forget to take out your trash and allow it to sit for a few days. The pile of fruit and vegetable peelings that sits on the top of the trash gives off a spectrum of smells as it rots. Many of us have experienced this natural (and often unpleasant) process in the comfort of our own apartments or homes.

The process of fermentation that takes place in your trash can is a form of controlled decomposition. It's an organic process carried out by microorganisms that feed upon an organic source for energy. With this in mind, we can make an interesting connection to the philosophy of the seasons: Decomposition is associated with death. An organic source dies, is broken down, and is subsequently used by other organisms. It is a necessary step in the circle of life. Decomposition takes place after the death of an organism and always precedes the genesis of new life. To put it simply, decomposition (and fermentation) is intimately related to the two universal seasons of life and death.

Each time we drink a beer, we are invited to reflect upon this natural cycle of life and death. *Each time we drink a beer, we are invited to reflect upon this natural cycle of life and death.* Without getting too "deep" or "depressing," we can say that fermentation is a microcosm of the season of death and a symbol of "dramatic beauty." Even the product of fermentation, an alcoholic beverage, can contribute to the celebration of life (a healthy buzz from intoxication) or a reflection on death (alcohol poisoning). As simple as it may sound, the beer in your hand reflects the season of life! Or, when beer is abused, it can give us a glimpse into the season of death. The fermented beverage in your hand is a profound symbol of the life cycle.

Hops: Four main ingredients go into every beer, but only three of them are necessary for production: water, barley, and yeast. The hop is the only ingredient in beer that is regularly used but is unnecessary for the chemical reaction of making alcohol.[39] So why do we add it?

The original purpose of adding hops was to keep beer fresh during long journeys; hops act as a natural preservative. The origin of adding hops to beer is associated with the style of beer known as the IPA (India Pale Ale). Great

Britain was sending troops to India and desired to bring beer on the journey to please the crewmen. Unfortunately, the journey took so long that most beer would spoil. The government asked brewers to think outside the box. They began experimenting with natural preservatives, but many of them made the beer unpalatable. They soon discovered that hops added a complementary flavor while making the beer last through the journey. Thus, the IPA was born.

Since then, newer methods of preservation, such as pasteurization (heating the beer to kill bacteria), have replaced the more natural method of using hops. Yet the hop remains an important component of brewing. Almost every beer contains some hop variety. The bitterness is used to balance a variety of malty, sweet, or sour notes. Although the use of this small green bud has shifted in purpose from health (preservation) to art (appreciation of bitterness), it still holds a special place in our hearts (and taste buds!). The hop has become a symbol of artistic appreciation.

Like fermentation, bitterness has often been associated with death. Look at Sacred Scripture. The writer of Sirach describes death as bitter: "O death, how bitter is the reminder of you" (Sir 41:1). Ecclesiastes compares death to a bitter flavor: "I discovered more bitter than death the woman whose heart is snares and nets, and whose hands are fetters" (Eccl 7:26). Lastly, Samuel makes the same comparison when he says, "Surely the bitterness of death is past" (1 Sm 15:32).

Bitterness and fermentation have the same effect on us: They force us to examine the season of death, which is a part of the cycle of life. Each cup of hoppy beer reminds us that beauty can be found in suffering.

This suffering, like bitterness, takes time to understand. Think about the first time a child tries coffee. His face tightens and he cringes. Even the most balanced cup of coffee can make us contort our faces. This is often the same reaction that young adults have when they try their first pale ale. Our natural reactions to each beverage reveal how we do not naturally enjoy bitterness. It is not an "obvious beauty." Rather, bitterness is an acquired taste. It reveals a "dramatic beauty," one that takes time, reflection, and understanding to fully appreciate. Like any acquired taste, we must come to accept it over time. Time is key.

* * *

I have made the case throughout this chapter that living according to the seasons, rather than becoming a snowbird, will lead us to greater fulfillment. The snowbird misses out on the most beautiful element of each season — namely, that which results from a transformation of suffering — whereas the seasonal person, who risks pain and bitterness, experiences both the obviously beautiful moments and the "dramatically beautiful" moments. She is able to reflect upon the entirety of her experiences, which range from suffering to joy. With these experiences in mind, she can transform her current worldview. She is well equipped to join or create a community, filled with friends of virtue, and experience future moments of suffering with the hope that joy is right around the corner.

In this context, beer is simply one symbol that helps us recognize the beauty right under our noses and the beauty that comes from suffering. *Beer is simply one symbol that helps us recognize the beauty right under our noses and the beauty that comes from suffering.* It is a good starting point for the average Christian, the saint in training. The drink in our hand teaches us that each IPA and each moment of suffering alike, shared in community, can become a moment of great fulfillment.

Up to this point we have focused primarily on transforming the suffering that we experience to feel true joy. I purposely avoided discussing joy because it demands its own chapter. In the following chapter, we will address the season that is familiar to anyone who has experienced an outburst of joy: the season of celebration.

Chapter Four

WHY DO YOU DRINK?

A THEOLOGY OF CELEBRATION

We must learn to celebrate. I say learn to celebrate,
because celebration is not just a spontaneous event. We have
to discover what celebration is.
JEAN VANIER, *FROM BROKENNESS TO COMMUNITY*

It is important to avoid the kind of celebrations
that really celebrate nothing.
RICHARD FOSTER, *CELEBRATION OF DISCIPLINE*

Sometimes we do things but never question why we do them. Seemingly absurd actions become traditions that we pass on to the next generations. These traditions often have little explanation, and we never think to question them.

In marriage, one spouse is grafted onto the family of the other and must embrace their traditions. For example, my wife's family introduced me to an annual tradition that has been a part of their family for many generations, farther back than any of them can remember. I'll share that tradition with you now. You'll probably think it's an odd tradition or hard to grasp.

The tradition begins each year when the weather gets cold and the final leaves have fallen from the trees. My wife's parents schedule the event a few weeks in advance so the whole family can prepare accordingly. The first year I experienced this tradition, it was in these preparatory weeks that things started to seem weird.

I began noticing a number of small changes within the daily activities of my in-laws. One morning, I caught my brother-in-law humming tunes under his breath as he made coffee. This was an unusual break from his pragmatic and systematic computer-programmer mystique. Then, my wife's aunt started to speak openly about her finances at dinner; her budget suddenly became public knowledge. My sisters-in-law were eating candy on a more frequent basis and, to top it all off, the younger cousins were well behaved! I asked, "Is there something in the air? What is this tradition about, anyway?"

The day finally arrived after weeks of anticipation. My wife and her family went outside, removed a healthy plant from the yard, and kept it inside the house for the next month. I assumed they were trying to protect it from the harsh weather.

The plant received a lot of attention over the following weeks. Sometimes I would walk in the room and catch my in-laws staring at it for no reason. They even went as far as decorating around the plant!

I tried to ask about the significance of the tradition, but nobody really seemed to know. The same reason was voiced time and time again: "We have always done it this way. It is important to us!"

Sounds crazy, right?

For those of you who have not caught on, I just described the popular tradition of finding, cutting down, and decorating a Christmas tree.

You have to admit: The whole thing sounds odd when

I put it this way. The act of killing a healthy tree does not make sense if you are an outsider to the tradition. (It hardly makes sense if you are an insider, but I won't get into that now.) Regardless, the tradition has become widely accepted by our culture. It is ingrained in our families, and it is rarely questioned.

* * *

We can learn a lot about our traditions when we take a step back and reflect upon them.

The first step in this process of reflection is the most important: We must demand an explanation for each tradition. As we receive some answers, we will discover that each familial, religious, or cultural tradition can teach us something important about our personal beliefs. We are given the opportunity to ask important questions:

- Does this tradition align with my beliefs?
- Is it important for the identity of my community?
- Does it bring me fulfillment, or does it make me feel empty?

Let's now turn our attention back to alcohol and ask these same questions about beer and the traditions that we associate with its consumption:

- Does drinking align with my beliefs?
- Is drinking alcohol important for the identity of my community?
- Does alcohol bring me fulfillment or leave me empty?

Asking the right questions and reflecting upon our drinking traditions can help us better understand what it truly means to celebrate and why we choose to drink. So the purpose of this chapter is to discuss the one season that should stand out for the average young adult: the season of celebration.

I bet that each one of us can agree, to some extent, that our current method of celebration leaves room for improvement. In response, I would like to provide an answer to the questions presented above. Theology offers us the means of transforming any experience into something that fulfills us and strengthens our community. We began to see this in the previous chapter when we analyzed the many ways that the seasons offer us new perspectives on life. Now, in this chapter, I want to apply this same answer to the way that we party. I want to discuss celebration through this seasonal lens. This season, celebration, offers us a great wealth of joy if we learn how to access it. Therefore, we must relearn how to celebrate.

Putting Celebration in the Hot Seat

Think back to the lesson of the Christmas tree: We learned that it is uncommon to question our traditions. In a similar way, we are not naturally prone to question our celebrations. To highlight this point, I ask my students, "Would you rather party, or talk about partying?" They almost unanimously respond with the former: "Let's party!"

Like many other areas in our lives, we act but fail to reflect on that action. We eat but rarely question what we are eating. We nap instead of reflecting on the importance of rest. We party instead of talking about celebrating.

This unexamined, action-centered approach can become problematic over time. For instance, what do we do when we gain weight and realize that our diet was never sustainable? What do we do when our celebrations become unfulfilling, but we have never learned how to question them? Some students shrug their shoulders and admit defeat: "It has always been this way, and there is no way to change it."

How would you respond?

Plato famously captured the words of Socrates who, in his final hours, expressed, "The unexamined life is not worth living" (*Apology*, 38a5–6). Following this dictum requires us not only to act genuinely, but to reflect upon our actions. Otherwise, according to Socrates, life is not worth living.

But changing the way that we celebrate (and think about celebrating) is a difficult task.

A simple first step is to consider how we respond to authority. How would you respond to the order "Don't do that!"? A common example that comes to mind is a parent telling a child not to eat a cookie out of a cookie jar. "Don't eat the cookies!" But, we have to ask ourselves, "Does this approach work?"

Normally, no. My third-grade waist size is proof.

Instead, it is natural for us to distance ourselves from an authoritative voice and even ignore the message. We may even become more likely to abuse something when we are told to avoid it. I ate three cookies instead of one because the object became a "forbidden fruit." I came to desire it more than before.

Directives against alcohol follow a similar pattern. Phrases such as "Don't drink underage" or "Don't binge drink" fall on deaf ears. Listeners are bound to respond to the commands by "drinking the fruit," often in excess.

Why isn't this approach effective?

It's difficult to instill in adults the desire to change behavior unless a better alternative is presented.[40] Contrast the two approaches: giving an order ("Don't do that!") or setting a higher standard ("You should do *x* instead, because it is more fulfilling!"). Think about how you would respond to each. Who would you listen to?

I cannot speak for young children, but it is more effective for teenagers and young adults to set a higher standard than to issue an order (often with a threat of punishment attached). Many of us would prefer to hear "You should drink in a fulfilling way!" rather than "Stop drinking!" This approach is more realistic, and frankly more human. We are the best versions of ourselves when we are seeking fulfillment rather than simply avoiding emptiness.

So drink up … but only if it fulfills you!

Finding Christ in Xmas

Christian writer and theologian Richard Foster warns his readers that "it is important to avoid the kind of celebrations that really celebrate nothing."[41] His statement assumes one important fact: We are always celebrating *something*. So our next question must be: What are we celebrating?

It is sometimes difficult to label exactly *what* we are celebrating at a party. Consider for a moment the common college party, or the last one that you attended. What was being celebrated?

Was it a person? Unlikely, unless it was a birthday.

Was it a momentous occasion? Most likely not.

Wait, was the party just a reason to drink? Bingo.

In light of this observation, we must translate Foster's statement from a warning to "avoid the kind of celebrations that really celebrate nothing" into a statement of encouragement. For the young adult in the modern world "it is important to fully engage with the kind of celebrations that really celebrate *someone* or *something*."[42]

Inspired by this statement, we must put each of our

parties on the hot seat and ask the important questions like "What am I celebrating?" and "Am I celebrating something, someone, or nothing?" Really think about it!

* * *

The American holiday is a perfect case study that can help us answer this question. Let's step back and reflect upon our use of language and the way that we refer to each holiday. We can quickly see that each popular American holiday has been renamed at some point in history to account for a growing trend. Observe this point in the following chart:

Original Name	Popular Name
Christmas	Xmas / "The Holidays"
Easter Triduum (Holy Thursday–Easter Sunday)	Hoppy Easter
Independence Day	Fourth of July
Thanksgiving	Turkey Day
Feast Day of St. Patrick	St. Paddy's Day
All Hallows' Eve	Halloween

The name changes reveal an important development in the celebration of holidays. We have begun to focus more on the actions associated with each holiday than the person or historical occasion for whom or about which the holiday was originally intended. Consider the following chart as a reminder of the person or event that was originally celebrated:

Original Name	Original Purpose
Christmas	Celebrate the birth of Jesus
Easter Triduum	Celebrate the Death and Resurrection of Jesus
Independence Day	Celebrate the adoption of the Declaration of Independence and the formation of a new nation
Thanksgiving	Profess gratitude for the people and blessings in our lives
Feast Day of St. Patrick	Recall the life of a saint who brought unity to Ireland
All Hallows' Eve	Recall and become inspired by the lives and actions of the saints who came before us

Secular culture has changed the purpose of each holiday to emphasize actions rather than people. Far more people associate beer and the color green with "St. Paddy's Day" than the impact Saint Patrick had on his country. The popular bumper sticker that inspires readers to "Keep Christ in Christmas" expresses the worry that Santa Claus has overshadowed Jesus. We are more prone to consume turkey, watch the parade, and fall asleep during a football game than give thanks to God and one another on Thanksgiving. In sum, the new holiday names (and the actions that accompany them) have become the norm rather than a fleeting trend. Consider the following:

Popular Name	Popular Purpose
Xmas	Open presents, sing carols, and eat food
Hoppy Easter	Egg hunt, find your basket, and eat candy
Fourth of July	Wear patriotic colors, drink beer, and shoot fireworks
Turkey Day	Watch a parade, eat turkey, and watch football
St. Paddy's Day	Wear green and drink green beer
Halloween	Scare people, dress up, and eat candy

As we can see, the original purpose of each holiday was to celebrate a person or a historical event. Christian holidays were particularly attentive to celebrating people: the life of Jesus or the lives of saints. The aim of these celebrations is to study, celebrate, and appreciate the extraordinary lives of other people. We can learn a great deal from these influential people, such as how to treat our neighbor, the earth, and our fellow Christians.

A concern must be addressed before we continue: It's a mistake to carry a false sense of nostalgia for "the way people celebrated in the past." Many Christians complain, "If only we could go back to the 'good ol' days' when children dressed up as saints for Halloween, and Christmas was all about Jesus!" In truth, the secular traditions have always been so thickly intertwined with the religious that making a complete delineation between the two is unrealistic. Holidays were never as holy as people imagine them to have been, even though the term holiday originated from "holy day." They were never perfect.

Rather than blind ourselves with an idealized past world, we should seek out small ways to transform our celebrations *within* the new traditions. The Christian mission must be broadened: It is just as important to "Find Christ in Xmas" as it is to "Keep Christ in Christmas." The vocation of each Christian is to transform the culture from within rather than impose reform from the outside. *The vocation of each Christian is to transform the culture from within rather than impose reform from the outside.*

Celebrate Good Times (and People), Come On!

My parents did a wonderful job teaching my brothers and me the importance of structured daily prayer. Each night, before we would retreat to the land of fluffy comforters and weird dreams, my family would gather in the living room for prayer time. I'm still impressed that the structure remained consistent for over twenty years:

1. Prayer leader invokes the Sign of the Cross.
2. Prayer leader chooses a traditional prayer or song — all pray or sing.
3. Prayers of Thanksgiving — take turns, youngest to oldest.
4. Requests for forgiveness — take turns.
5. Prayers of Petition — take turns.
6. Prayer leader closes in the Sign of the Cross.

The role of prayer leader would rotate each night. Each one of us had a different "go-to" prayer or song; mine was the prayer of greatest brevity (the Glory Be) or, if I wasn't in a hurry, the Celtic Alleluia.*

The leader was also responsible for asking the questions that prompted numbers 3–5. In my words, they were as follows:

---

* Imagine a makeshift choir of middle-school boys (my brothers and me) singing, "Hale-Hale-Hale-LUUUUUUJAAAAAAHHH!" (*with clapping*).

1. What are you thankful for?
2. What do you confess?
3. What do you pray for?

My dad, one of the founders of nightly prayer time, would pose the questions a bit differently than the rest of us. He asked the third question: "For whom or what would you like to pray?" Not only was his grammar more correct; he was asking an entirely different question. But we never caught on.

My brothers and I would fumble, night after night, through the same set of responses: "I pray that we sleep well tonight, have a good day at school tomorrow, and that tennis practice goes well. We pray to the Lord." This trend remained consistent for most of our childhood years. We answered his question. Or at least what we thought was the question. It wasn't until many years later that our dad shared with us a hard truth: We answered only the easy part of his question!

My older brothers and I, during recent visits home, admire the maturity of our youngest brother. Nolan, who is still in high school, takes a completely different approach to answering Dad's question. Rather than praying for activities, answering the "what" of the question, Nolan lists off the names of people who are in need of prayer. His prayer is personalized. He is forced, each night during prayer, to come *face to face with the people for whom he prays*. Intention is everything. He prays with the hope that people other than himself will be affected by the grace of God. It is a selfless request to God, unlike our usual self-centered demands.

How #11: Give Your Prayer a Face. Make Prayer Personal.

Turn to page 162.

My dad's question, "For whom or what do you pray?" taught my brothers and me two things about our human nature and the nature of celebration:

- First, it is harder to pray for someone than it is to pray for something. Personalizing prayer takes more time and effort than asking God that our personal actions will end in success. At the time, I took this lesson back to college and applied it to the party culture. This led me to discover the second point:
- It is harder to *celebrate someone* than it is to *celebrate an activity.* Most of us would readily admit that celebrating a person takes more effort than focusing on ourselves. It is easier to stay in my own world and drink beer, dance, or play drinking games.

During family prayer nights growing up, the prayers that I made for the activities of the following day were comfortable and easy to recite without a second thought. I never had to think outside of my own situation or leave the comfort of my armchair. Each night I became more centered on myself and less interested in others. I allowed the "for whom" of my dad's question to become overshadowed by the "for what."

How often does our prayer and our experience of celebration fall into the same trap?

In the following section I will introduce you to a few more characters who need to make an appearance on the playbill that we started in the previous chapter. Their roles at a party are integral to understanding the ways that we celebrate.

Takers: "What Can I Get from This?"

Engaged couples who are preparing to get married in the Catholic Church are required to meet with a priest to discuss their reasons for getting married. These initial conversations provide a launchpad for the couple as they start to learn about the spiritual depth of the Sacrament.

A few years ago, as my wife and I inched closer to our wedding day, the time came for us to fulfill this requirement. We scheduled a meeting with Father Satish, our parish priest at the time, and prepared accordingly. With baptismal certificates in hand, we made our way across town to Immaculate Conception Parish.

Our arrival at the parish center was announced by the bark of a small white dog. Then, Father Satish, a middle-aged priest from India who sports an iconic ponytail, greeted us in the foyer and led us back into his office. Kayla and I sank into his comfortable black-leather armchairs and began to answer a barrage of questions.

About midway through the conversation, Father Satish paused. An uncomfortable silence filled the air, only to be broken a moment later by a question. What he said next will be forever ingrained in our minds.

He asked, "Do you want to know the number one reason why couples get divorced?"

Kayla and I both responded with shared enthusiasm, "Well yes, of course, please tell us!"

Father continued, "I'll tell you the secret. It's quite simple, actually: Divorces are bound to happen when one partner looks at the other and says, 'What can I get from you?' instead of 'What can I give you?' As long as you keep asking 'What can I give you?' your marriage will last."

We have found that the advice from Father Satish is not confined to marriage alone; it applies to almost any situation in life. Our entire lives can change if we begin to ask "What can I bring to this?" instead of always asking

"What can I get from this?" We can refocus our attention from the "self" to the "other," from taking to giving.

To be more specific, we can pose Father Satish's question each time we attend a celebration or a party because, when it's all boiled down, marriage and celebration share a great deal in common. In a certain sense, marriage is one long celebration because spouses are called to give to one another until death. But this is not a book on marriage. This is a book on celebration! To see the practical implications of these questions, let us observe two hypothetical parties that embody each.

Imagine attending a party that is packed with people who share the mindset "What can I get from this?" A familiar scene begins to unfold: The beer, probably a low-quality domestic beer, runs out quickly. A bag of chips and a cup of salsa that were set out by the host are devoured within seconds. The dance floor is full of single people looking for dance partners, a smattering of lonely hearts taking turns dancing with strangers. As the bass-heavy music dies down, and the lights go on, we can faintly make out a crowd of people who were formerly unacquainted, leaving together in pairs. The "lucky" few have found sexual partners they can take home for the night. The "What can I get from this?" continues into the early hours of the morning.

Anyone observing this party is faced with an alarming truth. It's natural for us in our unrefined nature to want everything in sight: beer, food, people, etc. Our end goal, in every activity, is personal pleasure.

Let us label these archetypal partygoers as "takers." A "good" party supplies the takers with adequate means of consumption, whereas a "bad" party fails to supply the takers with their "wants." Simply listen to the comments that are shared over brunch the morning after a party to better understand how young adults rate their experiences.

Each party receives a grade, expressed in phrases such as "That party sucked!" or "Man, that was an awesome party." These judgments are based on the amount of alcohol, food, or people that were available for the taking.

In this setting, everything and everyone is at risk of becoming an object that can be taken for personal pleasure. We quantitatively talk about how many beers we drank, how much free stuff we received, and how many people we danced with. Takers are obsessed with quantity and consumption, and they can be compared to children who count their candy after trick-or-treating on Halloween:

"How much candy did you get?"
"I got forty pieces, how about you?"
"I got sixty!"
"Man, I'm jealous! Hopefully, next year is better."

How #12: Use Qualitative Language to Rate a Party.
Turn to page 164.

The stereotypical description of a party that I've used thus far is narrow and stingy. I have purposely given an extreme example (an archetype) to illustrate what can happen when we foster the mindset "What can I get from this?" Extreme examples like this help us understand and avoid possible risks. These risks directly influence a number of relationships:

- A community of takers risks divorce, not in a marital sense, but in a communal sense.
- The number of divisions in a community will increase when consumption overshadows community.

- Fallouts between friends occur more frequently because there is a constant pressure to provide the goods necessary for pleasurable taking.
- Friends of pleasure risk being replaced on a whim by others who have greater access to pleasurable goods.

The purpose of a celebration is also prone to become self-centered if there is no other person (Jesus, a saint, a friend, etc.) who is being celebrated. When we think that a party is about us (taking), we can be physically present but fail to develop an authentic sense of community. It's easy to ignore the people around us as we focus on ourselves. The entire party risks deteriorating into a mere gathering of isolated agents when each person in attendance has this same mindset. Jean Vanier describes an experience of watching people dance at a nightclub: "It was amazing; there was no togetherness. ... It seemed as if each one was jogging up and down all alone!" He responds, "Somehow we need to rediscover what dance and celebration are."[43]

Now let us paint a picture of the opposite extreme. Imagine attending a party full of people who share the mindset "What can I bring to this?" The refrigerator overflows with craft beer that is intended for sharing. The playlist encourages good vibes and is conducive to conversation rather than promiscuous dancing. Bags of chips, small appetizers, and other snacks adorn the table. Friends bring other friends and introduce them to one another to broaden the community of virtue. Conversation is rich with jokes and stories that bring people together.

You are probably asking yourself: "Where can I find such a party?"

Let me warn you: Finding a party that fits this mold should not be our primary concern. We will likely become discouraged in the face of the many parties out there that fail to match our criteria. Instead, the key to finding a ful-filling party is finding the right people with whom we can celebrate.

So who are these people?

Givers: The Artists of Celebration

Recall from Chapter 2 how humans will take any regular activity and, over time, turn it into an art. We followed the examples of clothing, architecture, and brewing, which were transformed from necessary trades to artistic crafts. Each one of these crafts became the means for humans to imitate God's creation and cocreate alongside God. In a sense, they elevated humanity. Now, with these examples in mind, we must introduce another craft that can be transformed into an art: celebration.

If we want to talk about art, then we must inevitably talk about artists, because every form of art must have an artist. A true artist embodies certain qualities that set her apart from every other person in the trade. What quality, therefore, sets apart the true artist of celebration from everyone else who parties?

You may have noticed that we already introduced the most important quality of the artist of celebration: having the mindset "What can I bring to this party?" The artist of celebration, at her core, is a giver. She is the nemesis of the taker.

The giver brings her gifts to the table and gives them freely. She anticipates the needs of others and desires to serve. The giver, who embodies the question "What can I bring to this?," celebrates people rather than actions. Recall the philosophy of friendship from Chapter 1. The giver views her friend as an end, not a means to an end. Giving becomes a condition for virtuous friendship. Thus, each virtuous friendship is shared between two givers. *Giving becomes a condition for virtuous friendship. Thus, each virtuous friendship is shared between two givers.*

The giver does not worry about taking, because she trusts that she will receive all that she needs as a result of her giving. We hear this in the popular prayer of Saint Francis, which proclaims the message: *"For it is in giving that we receive,* it is in pardoning that we are pardoned, and it is in dying that we are born to eternal life."

But wait, you may be thinking, this seems paradoxical. How will I end up with more if my goal is to give away all that I have? Well, a relationship between two givers is fruitful for both people. We receive what our friend gives, and our friend receives what we give. This noncapitalistic "exchange" is a true economy of gift-giving. Everyone wins! It is truly in giving that we receive.

We must also remember that the focus of a giver is the person who is with her, not the action that is being performed between them. She celebrates people, not actions. An action might play an important role in the celebration, but it is never allowed to overshadow the people who are present. And, between people, a gift from one friend to the other becomes more than a nice gesture or an exchange of goods; it is a celebration of a person.

We can summarize the life of a celebratory giver by rephrasing the prayer quoted above. "For it is in giving that we are *fulfilled.*" Although it seems paradoxical, a night of giving will leave our soul feeling fulfilled in ways that are hard to explain.

From Givers to Takers

We must balance our newfound desire to be givers with a hard truth: Humans are naturally prone to be takers because taking feels good in the moment and provides instant gratification. Taking is also efficient and inexpensive. For example, ripping shots of cheap liquor is the easiest way to reach intoxication. It is cheaper and less time-consuming than sharing a craft beer with a friend. A similar example can be found in the hookup culture. Young adults are more likely to invest a few hours in sexual gratification than years in a relationship that may cause discomfort, pain, or heartbreak. Both of these, the hookup culture and the drinking culture, share the same source: the Fall. We are naturally self-centered beings who are prone to taking.

Our self-centeredness can become an epidemic if it is left unaided. Society tells us to take, so we take. We are told to consume, so we consume. After enough time our habitual consumption becomes mechanical. We become enslaved to our consumption.

The first responders to this epidemic are ethicists, theologians, and counselors who ask the question: How do we keep our human tendency to "take" from spreading?

One answer can be found in the famous twelve-step program. Each variation of the program starts with the same step: Recognize and say that there is a problem.

The first step to finding a cure to our self-centered nature is recognizing that we have this natural tendency to make self-centered decisions. Our path to becoming "givers" can begin only once we realize that we are "takers."

But the cure is costly; the choice to become a giver is countercultural and inefficient. It will always be met with resistance. Society pressures us to consume and take rather than give of ourselves.

That is where our second step comes in.

The second step follows this logic: If celebration is an art, then it requires practice, like every other form of art. Instead of promoting abstinence, we must *learn how to celebrate*. We must practice the art of celebrating.

Luckily enough, all of us are able to celebrate, which means that all of us are able to practice. Celebration is unlike other forms of art that require expensive resources and hours of practice (brewing, architecture, music, dance, etc.). In it, we all have the opportunity to practice our trade and engage in more fulfilling celebrations. As young adults, we are frequently given the opportunities to practice giving to our community rather than taking from it. Each weekend is an opportunity to practice our art!

A final comparison may prove helpful for accepting our malady and striving for a cure: The process of becoming an artist of celebration is like the process of becoming a friend of virtue. Masters of the craft (Chapter 1) teach us how to truly celebrate by word and by example. We imitate the archetypes of the Christian family (Jesus, Mary, and the saints) or the people in our community (mentors, friends of virtue, etc.) who give generously of their time, energy, and resources.

We will quickly learn from these examples that the mindset of giving is contagious. It begins with one person who is selfless enough to give rather than take. Then, it spreads to the entire community. A new epidemic will break out when we learn how to name the problem at hand; an epidemic of giving can cure the epidemic of taking.

Saint Francis the Streaker

Do you know the story of Saint Francis of Assisi? If you know anything about him, what image comes to mind? A cracked, moss-covered statue in a yard, maybe. Or a picture of a man, clad in brown, frolicking through a forest. You might even picture a "Snow White" Saint Francis, talking to the bird on his shoulder.

But any accurate biography of the saint will reveal a different and somewhat humorous image that is far removed from the "Birdbath" Saint Francis or "Snow White" Saint Francis.

When he first decided to dedicate his life to something more than wealth and parties, the zealous young Saint Francis, filled with the Holy Spirit, ran *naked* through the streets of Assisi.

Yes, naked.

What was the occasion?

Well, Francis's father was a textile owner who gained his wealth by selling fabric. Francis, who shared his father's affluence and status, decided to renounce his father's wealth and challenge the social order. Renouncing his father's wealth also included renouncing the source of his wealth: clothing. He realized how wealthy he was and sought to distance himself from it, both physically and symbolically. He threw aside his life of comfort (and his cloak)!

Teachers and catechists share this story with Christians of all ages in hopes of inspiring self-reflection; they ask: "What do you need to 'give up' in your life?"

Their message is renunciation: cutting off the excess. This common reflection can lead to beautiful results.

But if we end the story here, as many people do, what are we left with?

A canonized streaker.

Saint Francis the Streaker has become the patron saint of renunciation and the face of modern Christianity. He embodies our obsession with getting rid of the things that stand between us and God. Retreat leaders preach to this anxiety and fill their talks with questions like: "What in my life gets in the way of my relationships with God and others?" "What sins should I stop committing?" "What should I get rid of?" At the end of the day, we are often left with nothing but bags of clothing to donate, an empty stomach, and the anxiety that we are not doing enough.

The spirit of Saint Francis the Streaker is resuscitated each year during Lent. He makes a guest appearance in Ash Wednesday homilies to remind us how to give up the things that distance us from God. We hear one question, repeated for forty days: "What are you giving up for

Lent?" One important misunderstanding lies behind this question: We are taught to think that Lent is only a dismal time of renunciation. We don our metaphorical sackcloth and ashes when we fast from chocolate, cake, or soda.

At this point some of you are saying, "Wait, you aren't telling the whole story!" Well, you are right. To finish the story of Saint Francis we must ask a follow-up question: Now that Saint Francis has renounced his life of wealth, status, and comfort, what is he free to do? Christians must ask the same question during Lent: Now that you are giving up *x*, *y*, or *z*, what are you doing *extra* for Lent? The answers to these questions indicate that our fasting during Lent and the renunciation of Saint Francis are not important in their own right. They are important because of the events that take place *after* and *because of* the fasting and renunciation. We fast so we can feast! Saint Francis renounced his father's wealth so he could announce the joy of the Gospel!

Renunciation only makes sense when it is balanced with annunciation. Fasting only makes sense when it is balanced with feasting.[44]

The story of Mary, immaculately conceived and sinless before God, is also incomplete if we talk only about her sinless nature. Her lifelong renunciation of evil and sin makes sense only after the Annunciation. Otherwise, she was just "that girl from Nazareth who didn't do anything wrong." The gift of freedom from sin enabled her to perfectly and wholeheartedly receive the Incarnate Word of God. Renunciation is only one half of a twofold conditioning of the soul. Renunciation allows Annunciation. *Renunciation is only one half of a twofold conditioning of the soul. Renunciation allows Annunciation.*

Feasting — what we have been calling "celebration" — is the liturgical season that corresponds to the season of fasting. These two seasons are microcosms of the two universal seasons, life and death, that we introduced in Chapter 3. We, as Christians, must remember that these two terms, fasting and feasting, are part of an exhaustive theological corpus that is alien to a secular audience. Our use of these terms must be prudent, and it is even more important that we translate them into a secular language. This is why "celebration" is so important: It is common ground between secular society and the spiritual life.

As we have started to see in this section, our search for a philosophy of celebration will unveil an important element of Christianity that is often overlooked or hidden beneath the facade of piety: Christianity has always been a religion of celebration. We must constantly remind ourselves that we, as Christians, must celebrate. It is who we are!

The Woman and the Leper

In 2015, the Christian folk band Rend Collective released an album titled *The Art of Celebration*. Each song follows a theme of faithful celebration, and the band pours their heart and soul into each live performance in an attempt to capture and spread a celebratory energy. A subtle message is spread to anyone who is lucky enough to hear the album or see them live: Christians must celebrate. Not only that, but they must strive to become artists of celebration.

The popularity of the term "celebration" in Christian conversations has decreased in recent years. Its zeal has been overcast by the shadow of silent piety. In our day, many Catholics think that a pious faith is lived on one's knees, representing a spiritual state of penitential sorrow. Simply look at the type of Christians who are held in highest esteem by the general population. We revere the saints who lived quiet lives in prayer and solitude. These individuals are heralded as "spiritual warriors" who lived the most honorable of lives, behind the scenes. Even religious images and icons capture their internal piety. We canonize

Mary and ignore Martha (Lk 10:38–42). In the silence of
the monastery we can hardly make out the whispers that
tell stories about the saints who celebrated.

Let me be clear: There is a proper time and place for
pious petition and contrition. It is an important season of
prayer! But just like the seasons of beer, and the four traditional seasons, there are more or less appropriate times
for each type of prayer. It is of utmost importance for each
Christian to discern the proper time and place for each
style of prayer.

We must first understand the various types of prayer,
our primary means of connection with God, before we can
discern the proper seasons for each. Christian theologians
have narrowed down four underlying reasons for why
Christians approach God in prayer: adoration, thanksgiving, contrition, and petition. The first two often take
the form of declarative statements. The second two are requests. Observe how the former are linked to celebration
whereas the latter are associated with contrition.

First, Christians pray in adoration. We treasure the
gifts of creation. These gifts include, but are not limited
to, the people around us, the natural world, and our ability
to cocreate with God. Adoration can take place within the
walls of a church or out in God's creation. True adoration
makes us care for ourselves, one another, and the world
around us. Everything is a gift to the Christian who lives
in a constant state of adoration.

Second, Christians give thanks to God. We reflect
upon the many blessings and graces in our lives and express our thanks to God. Each prayer is like a thank-you
card.

Both these actions, adoration and thanksgiving, are
associated with joyful celebration.

Third, Christians ask God for contrition. We approach God, a forgiving parent, who wants us to under-

stand our flaws and work to improve them. Contrition is often associated with guilt, feeling sorry, shedding tears, and the Sacrament of Reconciliation. It is a painful process of self-awareness that helps to strengthen the soul; we become like tempered steel, which, in being removed from the flame and plunged into water, is hardened.

Fourth, Christians appeal to the power of God and offer petitions. We want God to consider our needs and our wants. Permission to ask God for the things we want comes from Scripture, which tells us that we need only knock and our prayers will be answered (Mt 7:7–8; Lk 11:9). Many Christians associate the word "prayer" exclusively with this type of prayer.

I have witnessed firsthand how the modern obsession with contrition and petition has overshadowed the celebratory prayers of adoration and thanksgiving. This became most apparent during a prayer group that I led during my first year as a college campus minister.

The group consisted of eight students who met weekly to form community, learn new styles of prayer, and grow closer to God. We structured each meeting according to the same agenda:

- 15 Minutes: Check in
- 30 Minutes: Try a new style of prayer
- 15 Minutes: Conclude with a period of shared intentions

During the final minutes, I would invite each student to offer a prayer of petition. These prayers followed a similar pattern: "I would like to pray for ... " followed by the name of a family member with an illness, an issue between roommates, or other common problems that are worthy of prayer. Each prayer seemed to imitate the Prayers of the Faithful during the Catholic Mass.

I made an observation after the third gathering: Our time of prayer left us feeling exhausted and hopeless. It was like reading the news; we walked away asking, "Is there anything good happening in the world?" I immediately set out to diagnose the situation. I reflected, "How can we balance our spiritual exhaustion with joy?"

The word "Eucharist" kept popping up in my life following the start of my search. I heard it in class, conversations with friends, and prayer. I thought to myself, "God, what are you trying to say?" Then it all began to make sense. A professor reminded my class how the term "Eucharist" comes from the Greek *eucharistia*, which means "thanksgiving." Aha! After some final consultation with my fellow ministers I decided to try something new the following week: praying with thanksgiving.

The structure of the prayer group remained the same until the final section. I began, "We are going to try something new tonight. We are going to balance our prayers of petition with prayers of thanksgiving. This may be uncomfortable and new for some of you, but it is hard to imagine that there is nothing in your life worth celebrating! Instead of starting your prayer with 'I would like to pray for ... ' I invite you to begin your prayer with 'I would like to offer a prayer of thanksgiving for. ... '"

The result was a balance between prayers of petition and prayers of thanksgiving. Our experience of prayer instilled in us a sense of hope while reinforcing a sense of longing. The students, along with myself, learned that a celebratory life of prayer is liberating.

This example of my prayer group illustrates a troubling reality: The spiritual well-being of modern Christianity is at risk. Like these students, many Christians spend so much time on their knees that they forget how to stand in praise and adoration. Songs and laughter have been replaced by tears and lamentations. Fasting overshadows feasting. As a result, our spiritual life suffers.

This incomplete ideology, so often represented by Saint Francis the Streaker, is also often represented by one character in Scripture: the woman in sin who washed Jesus' feet with her tears (Lk 7:38). None of us can deny that her humility is inspiring. Her prayer, one of contrition, is powerful. But, we must also ask: Do we expend all our energy in washing the feet of Christ, so that we never join him at the table? Do we ever truly arrive at the feast? Many of us are guilty of narrowly imitating this woman. We have become deaf to the teaching of Saint Gregory Nazianzen, Church Father, who said: "We celebrate not our sickness but our cure."[45] We wash Jesus' feet with such tunnel vision that we forget to stand and look him in the eyes.

Jean Vanier invites us to reflect on this narrow imitation. He explains: "When I visit communities, I frequently ask, 'How do you celebrate?' If they say, 'We don't celebrate,' then I know the community risks death." [46] Whoa. The question of balancing prayer is not simply about making God happy: The entire Christian life is on the line!

Thankfully, Sacred Scripture offers us another character to balance the scales. This new character teaches us about the other half of a balanced life of prayer: adoration and thanksgiving. Recall the story of the tenth leper who, after Jesus healed him, "turned back, praising God in a loud voice" (Lk 17:11–19). He turned, realizing that he had been healed, and ran to Jesus with words of thanksgiving.

Jesus took note: "Were not ten cleansed? Where are the nine?" The other nine lepers continued with their lives, sleepwalking away from Jesus. They are the Christians who receive the Sacrament of Reconciliation and simply walk away. Are they still healed? Of course. But these nine represent the many Christians who suffer from a narrow faith. They never return to Jesus with words of thanksgiving.

How #13: Consider the Nonverbals of Prayer.

Turn to page 165.

We must always remember the words that Jesus offered a leper. He exclaimed, "Your faith has made you well" (Lk 17:19). In this moment, the leper shows us that "faith" should not be confined to repentance alone. When we leave faith at that, we fail to account for the many other seasons in our lives — the seasons that instill in us a deep sense of adoration, thanksgiving, or petition.

Faith, properly defined in this context, is a holistic balance of every means by which we communicate with God. Each Christian must prudently discern which style of prayer is most appropriate in each setting. On our own it can be difficult. But thankfully, the Church has provided a prime example to teach the Christian community how to balance each type of prayer. This example is the Mass, the liturgy.

Eucharistic Party Favors

Many Christians misunderstand the purpose of the Mass and either (a) complain that it is boring, or (b) stop attending.

The same complaint is voiced time and time again: "I don't get anything out of Mass!"

Comparing the Eucharistic celebration to a party may help us develop a newfound respect for the Mass. Just like a fulfilling party, the point of Mass is not to "get something" out of it. It is to offer ourselves and our gifts. The point of Mass is not to "get something" but to "give something."

How #14: Compare the Catholic Mass to a College Party.

Turn to page 167.

A rudimentary understanding of liturgical theology will help us explain this radical concept. Let us review the topic and get on the same page with a brief crash course.

According to the *Catechism of the Catholic Church*, each person who shows up at Mass and sits in the pew receives certain graces for simply being there and receiving the Eucharist. Liturgists at the Council of Trent gave this a fancy Latin name: *ex opere operato* ("from the work performed"). This means that the Sacraments derive their power from Christ's work, the "work performed," not by human efforts. In a sense, it is a safety net. The Sacrament retains its power to confer grace even if the priest and all the people gathered choose to ignore or reject the grace that is offered. The teaching of *ex opere operato* allows us to respect and honor the work of Christ while taking into account our human tendency to make mistakes.

But it would be unfair to discuss this teaching without addressing the frustration that it has caused in the Christian community. Consider the following: If everyone who receives the Eucharist receives the same baseline amount of grace, then what is the point of engaging in the celebration?

For example, one person can be visibly invested in trying to encounter Christ in the Eucharist. We can see her singing the hymns, responding with zeal, and giving freely at the collection. Two seats down, her roommate can be heard snoring in the pew, engaging only during the moments when she is jolted awake by the communal responses.

We must ask: Does one roommate receive more grace than the other? According to *ex opere operato*, both receive the same baseline amount of grace from the Sacrament.

I like to call these graces "Eucharistic Party Favors." You get one for just showing up, but you must wait until the end to receive it. Per Catholic theology, these "party-favor" graces may be sufficient to keep a soul alive, but they are not enough to help the soul thrive.

Yet as artists of celebration, we must remember that celebration is about thriving, not surviving. *Celebration is about thriving, not surviving.*

The teaching of *ex opere operato* has one major shortcoming for young adults: It fails to consider the human (and allegedly young-adult) desire to seek the route that is most efficient and least time-consuming. When given the chance, we will, almost always, choose the easiest option. For instance, if we learn that we can still get an A in a class by reading infrequently and doing the bare minimum for assignments, we will probably choose this option over the option that requires more work for the same grade. If our manager offers to give us fewer projects for the same pay, we will likely accept it without question.

As a result, liturgical celebrations are bound to suffer when Christians rely solely on the teaching *ex opere operato.*

Let us follow a person who takes advantage of *ex opere operato* along each moment of the liturgy and learn from his experience. Each action of the liturgy seems to be a time-consuming hurdle that he must jump before reaching the most important action: receiving the Eucharist. He purposely chooses not to sing and stands with his book held limp in his hands. The Liturgy of the Word, led by the priest and the lectors, is yet another part of the track that he must run. He hopes, each Sunday morning, that the homily will be succinct and to the point. After it concludes, he offers the sign of peace reluctantly with a forced smile. "So close to the end," he thinks. Finally, the time comes to stand up and process toward the altar. He ignores the community around him as he blindly steps forward.

The line is long, moving at an unbearably slow pace.

The sight of this man, waiting in line for the Eucharist, reminds us of an image from a party. It is comparable to the image of a college student in a crowded basement waiting in line for a keg. He slowly moves forward in line, empty cup in hand, and ignores the noise and bodies around him. He gets what he came for and returns to drinking. Both characters, the man in the Eucharistic procession and the man in the basement, misunderstand the purpose of their respective celebrations. They get what they came for, ignore the people around them, return home, and continue living as if nothing changed.

The way we consume beer and the way we consume the Eucharist can often be all too similar. Take, for example, the man who attends Mass and views the Host as a small piece of bread that is to be consumed simply to make him a better person. This character can be likened to the student who views the beer at a party as a cheap consumable that helps him reach intoxication. As absurd as it sounds, many of us are prone to think this way about Mass: Receiving the Eucharist is like getting your weekly time card punched. Everyone is doing it, which means that I should, too. We can get this card punched only if we sit through the entire service. Anything less is incomplete. Anything more is unnecessary. We punch the same time card at a party, because drinking beer is the accepted and proper weekend activity.

This young adult (who represents many Christians) misunderstands the purpose of the liturgical celebration. The Eucharist is not simply bread and wine that feeds our soul. It is not a time card or a party favor. Rather, Christians call this moment "Communion" because the recipient (the communicant) enters into communion with the Trinity and the entire Christian community. Following the transitive property (if a = b and b = c, then a = c), each person who enters communion with Jesus enters communion with others. Jesus is the source of communion. He is the gate for the sheep, through which we must all pass to join a community (Jn 10:7–10). He is the vine, and we are the branches (Jn 15:1–17). Through him, we become a community.

The major problem that Catholics face when it comes to liturgical celebration can be summed up in one question: How do we retain the reverence of the liturgy while celebrating the joy of the Resurrection? On the one hand, we know that something needs to be done. People are falling asleep in the pews. On the other, it is essential to sustain the tradition of the liturgy and avoid lapsing into a secularized shadow of true celebration.

Rather than asking the Church to make a major change, such as calling a Third Vatican Council, we should ask ourselves, the Christians who fill the pews, to make a change. Each Christian must personally ask, "Do I experience the joy of the Resurrection at Mass like it is a true celebration? If so, do I authentically show it? If not, how can I contribute to the celebration and bring the joy of the Gospel to life?"

A simple mindset change can enhance both our celebration of the Eucharist and our celebration at a party. Imagine if each person who attended Mass came with the mindset "What can I bring to this?" instead of "What can I get out of this?" People would greet their friends, family, and those around them with hospitable smiles before and after the celebration. The choirs of joyful song would fill the steeples. The "Amen" and "Alleluia" would shake the stained-glass windows with conviction. Collection baskets and bins would be filled to the brim with donations for those in need.

Doesn't this sound like a party you would like to attend?

We must remember that each one of us will express

our Easter joy in a different way, and in differing capacities. But for any of us, it is easy to start with small things. Smile. Greet those around you. Sing with your pew neighbor. Always remember the story of the widow: She teaches us that the one who gives generously, even if it is an offering of two coins, "has put in more than all of them" (Lk 21:1–4).

How #15: Give Your Time, Talent, and Treasure.
Turn to page 168.

The Eucharist is not simply an activity of reception. It is a face-to-face encounter with Jesus and, through him, the Father and Holy Spirit, as well as a communal act of thanksgiving (*eucharistia*) for the people with whom we celebrate. It is a celebration of people, not a celebration of actions. *The Eucharist is a celebration of people, not a celebration of actions.* The Holy Trinity is present. All the angels, saints, and souls in heaven are present. And, most frequently overlooked, the entire Catholic community on earth is present. In this moment of celebration, we must remember that "we are what we eat." We become the Body of Christ for one another and for the world.

Postcelebration Confusion
The blocks of time that come before and after a party are often as important as the party itself. Prior to the gathering we prepare ourselves mentally and spiritually for the conversations and fellowship that will be shared. Beer and food are purchased at local stores and a playlist is chosen. We lay the primer for the piece of art that the celebration will paint.

But what about the time after a celebration?

What do we do when a party is over?

Think about Christmas morning. For most of you, the thought of Christmas morning will evoke any number of positive emotions. We feel nostalgic when we remember ourselves as children, running into the living room to see the tree surrounded by gifts. The sounds, smells, sights, and feelings associated with the Santa Claus tradition take us back to this moment.

Let me share my experience of Christmas as a child. My family has a unique Christmas morning tradition that's unlike any other tradition I have seen. I'd always thought the tradition had existed since before I was born, and only recently did I learn that it was a more recent invention. (Don't worry; this isn't a trick like the Christmas-tree story.)

When we were younger, my parents allowed my brothers and I to open all our presents in one sitting, as many families do. Mountains of wrapping paper lay waste on the living room floor as we tore through the small veils between us and our new toys. We quickly analyzed each gift, reading the back of the box or giving it the ceremonial shake, before moving on to the next package. After about half an hour of tearing and shredding, my parents would leave the room to begin cooking our annual Christmas breakfast, leaving us to our new toys.

One year, when I was seven, my mom returned to the room and saw that our attention was occupied elsewhere. None of us were playing with our new toys. Instead, the television was on and all of us were feet away from the screen, absorbed in the program. Our presents lay behind us as we engaged with the show.

My parents, frustrated and confused by our lack of interest, diagnosed the situation. Here is what they observed: Our attention was lost once the shared activity came to an end. The last present marked the end of our Christmas community and the beginning of our search for other things to occupy us. We became confused when the shared activity ended, and then we sought a new action to keep us together. The television program, a new shared activity, was more appealing than playing in solitude with our new toys.

I would like to give a name to my parents' diagnosis: *postcelebration confusion*. We became confused when the perceived reason for celebration (opening presents) came to an end. This diagnosis can be universally applied to any celebration and can be found during most American holidays. For example:

- What happens on Independence Day after the fireworks finale? People pack up their chairs and coolers and return home. Or they find more fireworks to shoot off.
- What happens when the beer supply at a party runs out? Partygoers return home, go on a beer run, or seek out another party that still has beer.
- What do children do after they open all of their Christmas gifts and don't want to play on their own? They watch television.

Our family has been following a new annual tradition ever since the television incident. My parents, putting their creative minds together, came up with a treatment to our confusion. They realized that we could avoid postcelebration confusion by making the activity of opening presents last all day.

Here is a description of our new (and current) tradition: First, we sit down and each take *one* present from under the tree. We sing a Christmas carol and then open that single present. Then, my dad sets a timer for forty-five minutes. We are required to enjoy that gift for the entire period of time. After the allotted time, we return to the tree and do it again. This lasts all morning and afternoon and normally concludes with dinner.

The original purpose of this tradition was to stretch out the time of the shared activity (opening presents) to keep us from getting distracted by other sources of pleasure (television). In this sense, our tradition is no better than going on a beer run to keep a party going after the keg runs dry. But I have noticed as we have grown older that the tradition has morphed. My brothers and I often find ourselves with one another rather than off in separate rooms playing with our gifts in solitude. We have changed from friends of pleasure, who could easily dispose of one less pleasurable activity for another more pleasurable activity, to friends of virtue, who simply want to be in the presence of one another.*

My brothers and I have voiced to our parents that we may not need the tradition any more. Our focus has changed from an action (opening presents) to people (being with one another). Despite our requests, they have chosen to keep the tradition as a reminder. It reminds us that the purpose of Christmas day is to celebrate the birth of Jesus and the lives of one another. The true present is the presence of those around us.

* * *

Postcelebration confusion is a spreading epidemic. It has a particularly strong presence on college campuses and needs treatment. I remember, as a new student, preparing for the night by asking around to figure out what parties were being hosted and where we should go to find beer. My buddies and I would schedule out the evening, taking into consideration when a party started and how many

---

* Also, as we get older, we realize that one can only appreciate a pair of socks for so long. Forty minutes is a stretch.

kegs they had. This allowed us to create a mental timetable for when we should leave one party and walk to the next. Our goal was to keep the evening going as long as possible. We did everything in our power to avoid the post-celebration confusion that resulted when the last keg ran out. At the time, our friendships of pleasure could not survive merely on conversation and the presence of one another. We required an activity.

One popular story from the Bible tells a similar narrative: the Wedding at Cana in the Gospel of John (2:1–12). Jesus and his disciples showed up at the party and started to celebrate the newly married couple. Then, a terrible thing happened. The wine ran out![47]

This seemingly small fact happened to be a big deal for a first-century Jewish couple on their wedding day. Historians tell us that Jewish wedding feasts would traditionally last as long as two to five days. The hosts were expected to provide an excess of wine for the entire length of the celebration, and anything less would be an embarrassment for the family and a disappointment for those gathered.

Thankfully, the honorary guest, Jesus, would begin his public ministry that day. Mary recognized the severity of the problem and encouraged her son to do something about it. Jesus, moved by her recommendation, invited the servants to fill up jars with water. The servant drew out a glass and handed it to the master of the feast. The master, confused and awestruck, informed the bridegroom, "Every man serves the good wine first; and when men have drunk freely, then the poor wine; but you have kept the good wine until now" (Jn 2:10). Jesus replaced the average wine with top-shelf wine.

As a result, those who were gathered could remain gathered. The problem of postcelebration confusion was avoided. Party on!

Bishop Robert Barron, in his philosophical treatise

The Priority of Christ, gives Jesus a telling title based on his actions at Cana: Jesus is the Gatherer. Barron starts his chapter by defining how the opposite of gathering is "scattering," which is an attribute of the evil one.[48] The Greek word *diabolos* means "scatterer." It is interesting to note that the word for sin in German, *sunde*, also carries the connotation of dividing. Original sin, therefore, was a radical moment of scattering when man and woman became distanced from each other and from God. The troubled history of the twelve tribes of Israel, burdened with sin and tempted by the *diabolos*, shows how divided God's people were from one another and from God before Christ came to earth to gather them.

The miraculous transformation of water into wine at Cana is a moment of great reversal. Jesus gathers rather than scatters. *The miraculous transformation of water into wine at Cana is a moment of great reversal. Jesus gathers rather than scatters.* "Because of Jesus' miracle, a large group of celebrants will continue to be gathered around a couple who have chosen to form, themselves, an intimate community for the rest of their lives."[49] Jesus provided the means necessary for people to remain gathered. His active ministry began with an act of gathering.

The action of Jesus, the Gatherer, was reflected in the example of my parents who extended the Christmas tradition of opening presents. My parents knew that the presents were simply a means of remaining gathered. In the same way, Jesus provided wine in order to keep people gathered together. He knew that the people who remained would inevitably end up celebrating the newly married couple, just like my brothers and I shifted our focus from the gifts to one another. The focus shifts from the activity to the people gathered, the intoxication of the wine to the intoxication of love and the Spirit

A New Vision of Celebration

Throughout this chapter, we have come face to face with the aspects of our celebrations that need improvement. In response, I propose a new vision of celebration that may help us avoid celebrating actions rather than people, taking rather than giving, and postcelebration confusion. The best way for me to share this vision is by sharing a story.

My dear friend Isaac celebrated his twenty-first birthday in 2014. Our cohort, responsible for planning his evening, asked him, "Isaac, what would be your ideal state at the end of the night?" Many students would respond with "blacked out" or "hooking up" as their end goals. But Isaac was unique; he understood celebration better than most of us. His response was iconic.

"I would love to end up in our kitchen, around two in the morning, surrounded by you guys, talking about some deep topic. I hope to have a solid buzz, but I want to remember the entire night. We can drink water, eat cheese and venison [staple foods in our Wisconsin-based community] and share stories from the night. Sound good?"

We kept his goal in mind as we prepared for his party and as the night progressed. After bar-close, around two in the morning, we picked up some deep-fried cheese curds and half-skipped, half-walked our way back to the house. We ended up in the kitchen, some of us perched on the counters, others on barstools, with a goofy few who braved the tile floor. The conversation varied. Some parts were serious. Other moments were marked with outbursts of laughter. But the whole experience was picturesque.

Every now and then I would glance over at Isaac. I saw the same thing each time I looked: He wore a grin that spread across the width of his face. "We did it," I thought. "We celebrated the life of Isaac."

After a few pints of water, we made our ways to our respective rooms. A final, "Happy birthday, Isaac!" marked the end of the night. My head hit the pillow and I was out like a light.

The following morning was just as joyous as the night before. We awoke, somewhat groggy and sleep-deprived, to a slew of refrigerated breakfast supplies that had been purchased the day before. The celebration continued! Smells of breakfast filled the kitchen as we slowly awoke with coffee cupped in our hands and smiles on our faces. I could think of no better way to start Isaac's twenty-second year of life.

* * *

One uncommon factor, among many others, separated this evening from the average college night: We remained gathered after the activity of drinking alcohol ended. Most friends scatter at bar-close. Others stick around until their bellies are filled with "drunk food." But Isaac desired something greater. He fought the myth of postcelebration confusion. His celebration continued as long as the community remained gathered, not simply as long as the drinking continued. His focus was not on the alcohol but on the people who gathered to celebrate with him.

We turned this evening into a weekly tradition. The goal each night was to return to the kitchen, slightly buzzed and hydrated, but most importantly, gathered as a community.

Isaac's birthday party taught our community an important lesson, and that lesson inspired me to write this book. Once a party of "takers" consumes everything, they must go find more things to consume. The evening ends when there is nothing left to take. But, a party of "givers" can last forever. The party is self-replenishing. An activity is not required for the gathering to continue. We require simply the presence of one another. Any additional activity

— hydrating with water, eating chunks of cheese, or sharing conversation — is a gift. Everything is gift.

In conclusion, we have learned that our celebrations should not end when the activity comes to an end. A Thanksgiving feast is not ruined for the friends of virtue who burn the turkey. Christmas is not over once the presents are opened and the fruitcake is devoured. Rather, we must realize that the subject of our celebration is the person right in front of us. *We must realize that the subject of our celebration is the person right in front of us.* So raise a glass, and toast to the people around you. Cheers!

How #16: Practice the Art of Toasting.
Turn to page 171.

Close Your Tab
At the end of life, the eternal Bartender will close your tab and hand you a bill. The charges will reflect each decision made during your earthly life and, I like to imagine, a list of questions will be used to calculate the damage done:

- With whom did you drink?
- What did you drink?
- What did you do when you drank?
- When did you drink?
- Why did you drink?
- How did you transform your drinking experience?

Our answers, seen through the eyes of our newly acquired "theological beer goggles" can reveal what we truly believe. We are given a glimpse into areas of our lives that might have been purposely neglected or ignorantly overlooked until now. So spend some time reflecting upon each question: How would you answer the eternal Bartender?

Heaven, the eternal celebration, is a state of unimaginable fulfillment. It even exceeds fullness, because fullness is an earthly unit of measurement. Fullness is simply the highest degree of fulfillment that we can rationally conceptualize during our time on earth.

The heavenly state, on the other hand, is a transformation of the earthly state. The same elements are retained, as we can see by the resurrected body of Jesus, but the entire state of existence differs. This is hard to conceptualize, so I invite you to bear with me through a final story.

One summer, when I was teaching catechism classes to children in the program *Totus Tuus*, a young child asked me, "Excuse me, Mr. Trevor, if we eat Jesus' body each week, won't we eventually run out of body to eat?" I thought to myself, "What a great question! Now, how do I explain to a student in third grade about the resurrected body of Jesus?" Like all teachers, I chose to make a comparison.

"Imagine you are handing out candy on Halloween. Eventually you will run out of candy, right? That is like our life on earth. Everything runs out. But imagine a world where, on Halloween, people would never run out of candy. They could keep giving forever! This is like how our life will be in heaven. Jesus' body is part of this heavenly world, which never runs out. It is special! He never runs out of love to give us!"

One quality in particular defines a heavenly body: It gives eternally, never reaching the point of exhaustion. Jesus' resurrected body is a foreshadowing of the state that we will all share. Just like his resurrected body, which is given to the whole world, we will never reach a limit on our giving.

So in the meantime, we must ask the final question of this book: How can I give the gift of myself, in an eternal manner, during my time here on earth?

Do not let the scope of this question overwhelm you. Rather, challenge yourself, each morning, with this question: What gift will I give the world today? Each response — an action or a gift, a talent or a treasure — will change the world. We can transform not only our drinking experiences, but the entire way we live.

Chapter Five

HOW CAN YOU TRANSFORM THE WAY YOU DRINK?

A LIST OF PRACTICAL ACTIONS

Welcome to the practical section of our study. At some point you may have asked yourself: What is the point of theology if it is not practical? This chapter is the classic "call to action" that concludes every retreat talk, motivational speech, or sermon. It is a follow-up to certain points made throughout the book. Here I will present several ways to practice living a fulfilling life, regardless of whether you choose to consume alcohol.

Recommendations

#0: Practice Run: Learn How to Use This Book!

#1: Plan and Execute a Road Trip with Friends.

#2: Go on a "Friend-date" with a "Friend-crush."

#3: Reflect: Which "Masters" Do You Serve?

#4: Would You Still Drink Alcohol If It Did Not Make You Intoxicated?

#5: Host a "Cheaper Beer" Sampling Party.

#6: Go on a Brewery Tour, Vineyard Tour, or Distillery Tour.

#7: Go to an Art Museum: Learn to Respect Abstract Art.

#8: Build-Your-Own-Six-Pack: Sample and Compare.

#9: Reflect on the Bread and Wine of the Eucharist.

#10: Learn the Seasons of Beer.

#11: Give Your Prayer a Face: Make Prayer Personal.

#12: Use Qualitative Language to Rate a Party.

#13: Consider the Nonverbals of Prayer.

#14: Compare the Catholic Mass to a Party.

#15: Give Your Time, Talent, and Treasure.

#16: Practice the Art of Toasting.

#0: Practice Run: Learn How to Use This Book!

Congrats, you made it! Welcome to the practice run. Now you can flip back to page 18 and continue on your merry way.

#1: Plan and Execute a Road Trip with Friends.

When finished, turn back to page 37.

The act of planning a road trip is easier than it may seem. All you need is a winter break or a week of paid time off, a GPS, and some connections. My best friend, Ryan, and I have traveled most of the continental United States over the course of three years. And the best part? We paid $0 for housing.

- **When?** If you are a student, then set aside the time: All college students have winter break. Spend a week at home with your family and then set out on December 27. Most breaks allow roughly one and a half to two and a half weeks for traveling. That is plenty of time! If you are finished with school and working, then plan during the evenings over Skype and pick any week in the future.

- **Where?** Decide where you want to go; pick a destination. Many tourist traps have become so because there was originally a beautiful landmark or climate that people desired to see. The location then became obscured or neglected by consumerism. These are places to go find! But here is the real challenge. Spend only a maximum of three or four full days at your destination. Remember that the journey is more important than the destination.
- **Who?** Make a master spreadsheet and plan early. You should start to plan as early as October for a December trip. Take out a map and split up the trip. Brainstorm the hometowns of friends, family, and friends of family. Mark where friends (of usefulness, pleasure, or virtue) live along the way. Try not to spend more than ten hours in the car at a time. Send messages to each friend or family member and ask for their hospitality. (The Apostle Paul did this before he visited a town. The book of Romans is a perfect example of pre-road-trip correspondence.) Post a picture of your trip on social media, tagging your hosts and hostesses and requesting further help if needed.
- **How?** Ask Santa for gas money. Ryan and I would estimate the travel costs prior to leaving. Then each of us would ask our parents for the gift of an experience rather than physical gifts. Depending on the trip and the price of gas, our total expenses ranged from $250 to $350 each. Food was also never an issue. Imagine a dozen families that are excited to host you. Each night we received a delicious feast that was unique to the geographic region.

- **What?** Plan your activities but leave room for spontaneity. One of the greatest joys of staying with locals is getting a free and personalized tour guide for each town. Ask them what they love about their city and let them show you. Bring some books, audio books, playlists, the Bible, a deck of cards, a Frisbee, and other simple hobbies. For example, we would set up our slackline at rest stops, between palm trees, on a mountain, or between rocks on the beach of the Pacific Ocean as the tide came in. We climbed a mountain, went skiing, saw the sunrise over the Atlantic and the sunset over the Pacific (not on the same day, of course), explored dozens of art museums, drank mead in a hot tub, smoked cigars on the Vegas strip, led a retreat in South Dakota, and went snorkeling, to name a few. Most importantly, I developed a friendship of virtue with my road-trip partner.

#2: Go on a "Friend-date" with a "Friend-crush."

When finished, turn back to page 44.

My undergraduate housemate, Isaac, introduced me to the term "friend-crush." He used it once in reference to a guy he had met once or twice around campus. Isaac explained how he admired the guy's optimism and enjoyed many of the same hobbies. Instead of a regular crush, which is driven by romantic interest, Isaac desired to become friends with his friend-crush (purely platonic).

Think about the people you see around campus but have never gotten to know. Do you look up to any of these people? Are any of them supercool? Do they have great taste in beer or wine? Do they have impeccable style? Do they radiate the joy of the Holy Spirit? Are they super passionate about a certain social justice issue? If so, I encourage you to find a mutual friend who knows that person. Invite that friend to a gathering and have him or her invite the "friend-crush." Sounds like middle school, right?

Engage in the same activity as your "friend-crush." Play darts at a bar, go out for ice cream, toss a Frisbee, kick back with some FIFA, or share a beer. Express to the other person how cool you think they are. Telling someone that you have a "friend-crush" on them can be a great compliment (if they know what it means, that is). Hopefully they won't be weirded out. If nothing else, it is a good conversation starter!

A few my "friend-crushes" have become close friends. Some naturally fizzle out, while others stay strong. You never know what will come from a "friend-crush!"

#3: Reflect: Which "Masters" Do You Serve?

When finished, turn back to page 48.

Jesus warned, "No one can serve two masters; for either he will hate the one and love the other, or he will be devoted to one and despise the other. You cannot serve God and mammon [wealth]" (Mt 6:24). Jesus challenged his followers and continues to challenge Christians today. He invites us to examine our lives and the values of our communities.

The criteria of each master vary according to our community and our influences. The student who can best hold her liquor, the beer-pong winner, the total abstainer, the straight-A student who still finds time to drink, etc. Some students will look for a master whose ideals resemble those of a parent or high school friend.

Spend some time in prayerful reflection about the question: Who or what do you serve? Jesus gives us two options regarding the "masters" in our lives: We are either enslaved, or we are empowered. We should seek out the former.

First, we must ask what enslaves us. Titus 3:3 explains, "For we ourselves were once foolish, disobedient, led astray, *slaves to various passions and pleasures,* passing our days in malice and envy, hated by men and hating one another." Reflect upon the "passions and pleasures" in your life that enslave you and leave you feeling empty. These "masters" can be numerous things. They are not limited to people in our lives; they can also be objects, emotional states, or financial desires. We must be careful in our discernment to avoid worshipping these objects or states, because an object should never be placed above a person in level of importance.

The "mammon" of Scripture, translated above as "wealth," is different for each person. We commonly hear about the "masters" of wealth, fame, or comfort. The "American Dream" is a master that some Americans serve. Whatever it is for each of us, we are warned to avoid these "mammon."

There are also several equally impactful "masters" in the lives of young adults that are overlooked. These may include popularity, intoxication, intellectual pride, and sexual prowess. In sum, "mammon" is any idol that we hold above God or community. It replaces God as the center of our worship.

Who or what are the "masters" in your life? How do they positively or negatively impact your life of discipleship?

#4: Would You Still Drink Alcohol If It Did Not Make You Intoxicated?
When finished, turn back to page 61.

This question is a great conversation starter. How would you answer this question? What do your friends think?

Each semester I pose this question to my class. Most college students find it difficult to answer. The common consensus is "No." They say that the idea of casually sipping on a cheap beer is absurd. Then I follow up with the question, "How about a mixed drink or a good craft beer?" Their answer changes almost immediately. "Oh, like a virgin mimosa? Or a margarita? That would still be good. Or a nonalcoholic craft beer? I could do that!"

Sure, this question is unrealistic. But, like many questions in philosophy, the way we answer the question can reveal our hidden motives behind why we drink and help us reflect on them. Is our desire for intoxication greater than our desire to appreciate the art form in our glass? Both desires, intoxication and appreciation, are real. But each time we drink we must ask ourselves, "Are my priorities balanced or out of whack? Am I drinking to get drunk? Or am I drinking to enjoy the art of the beverage, the people I am with, and, as a result, feel the effects of intoxication?"

#5: Host a "Cheaper Beer" Sampling Party.
When finished, turn back to page 62.

When finished, turn back to page 62.

One of the major factors that deter college students from purchasing better alcohol is price. Cheap beer is cheap. Craft beer is not (as cheap). Anyone who has hosted a party knows this. It is more cost-efficient to purchase cheaper beer when you want to be generous and provide drinks for your guests. Many gatherings among young adults are conducted in this way. There are not a lot of potlucks or opportunities to "BYOB."

I want to introduce a new, slightly less economic but equally efficient way of thinking. It is possible to throw a good party without breaking the bank, and we can encourage a degree of artistic appreciation without spending our entire paychecks on craft beer. The best way to do this is to have a "cheaper beer" sampling party to learn which cheaper beers are enjoyable. It's mistaken to assume that all cheap beer is the same. Some are better than others!

Most college campuses or cities have a "standard" cheap beer that is associated with large parties. We must first disassociate ourselves from that beverage. (While I was there, Marquette University students tended to prefer Keystone Light, whereas University of Dayton students preferred Natural Light. Similarly, Iron City Light is popular in Pittsburgh, Hudepohl 14-K is big in Cincinnati, and Pabst Blue Ribbon is coveted in Milwaukee.) Next, we must gather a small group of friends and go to the liquor store. It is time to do some window-shopping. See which beers are comparable in price or cost a few dollars more than the campus or city "standard." Pick up a few cans of each and conduct a tasting. Decide as a community which cheaper beer suits your taste and is within your price range.

My friends and I underwent an evolution of "cheaper" beers during our undergraduate years. We switched from Keystone Light (the campus "standard"), to Hamms, to Pabst Blue Ribbon. We discovered that a small change in cost can transform a watery beverage, created for the sake of intoxication, into a beer that can be enjoyed with dinner, at the lake, around a campfire, or at a party. Sure, it is still incomparable to craft beer. But it makes hosting easier on your wallet and more pleasurable on your taste buds!

#6: Go on a Brewery Tour, Vineyard Tour, or Distillery Tour.

When finished, turn back to page 64.

Hospitality and art go hand in hand. Brewers, vintners, and

distillers alike welcome visitors on tours of their facilities and invite them to sample their products. We get to touch the vats and smell the wort. Both the process and product are explained in depth. The veil of mystery is removed.

Companies that create a quality product are usually excited to show off their production processes. Go online and research nearby breweries, wineries, or distilleries. A company's website will normally list available times for public tours and the respective costs. Get a group of friends together and sign up for one! A tour is a great way to become educated about the alcohol-making process and sample the entire portfolio of a brewer. Our appreciation for the product grows in tandem with our understanding of the process.

A tour is also the perfect social outing. A group of friends can meet for dinner and then continue the night at a brewery before hitting up the bars, or a couple can make the tour a part of a fun date night. No matter the circumstance, a community of appreciation can grow out of a tour. The shared knowledge of the process and appreciation of the product can spark conversation and lead to future gatherings.

Most tours include the additional perk of free samples. The company wants you to sample their craft. It's like an artist walking you through her gallery. She wants you to enjoy her hard work and creativity.

A tour also enables you to ask questions about the beer. The brewmasters are normally around during the tours and are a great source of knowledge. Most tour guides encourage you to ask questions. Take advantage of this luxury! Ask what sets them apart from other breweries. What was the creative process that went into crafting this beer? Are there any beers that they are in the process of perfecting? The next time you are at a bar or a liquor store, you can look for the beer that you enjoyed and recommend it to a friend.

#7: Go to an Art Museum: Learn to Respect Abstract Art.

When finished, turn back to page 66.

It's hard to walk into the abstract- or modern-art section of a museum and avoid saying, "This is art? I could do this!" Whenever I hear that, I'm tempted to respond, "Then why don't you?" I have never received a good response.

I think many people don't like modern art because it is something they can't understand at first glance. It takes time and, often, an explanation. A section from Annie Dillard's book, *The Writing Life*, encourages us to think about art in a new way: "Push it. Examine all things intensely and relentlessly. Probe and search each object in a piece of art. Do not leave it, do not course over it, as if it were understood, but instead follow it down until you see it in the mystery of its own specificity and strength."[50] Study these words of wisdom, and keep them in mind when you consume art.

Abstract art has a home within one philosophy of art, titled the art narrative. A narrative philosopher believes that each work of art is in conversation with the works that came before it and that will come after it. The artist joins an ancient conversation among artists from every century and every geographic location. Each piece is an attempt to "say something" or make an argument in response to what came before. It may challenge the social norm or contribute to it. It may break out of the box or color within the lines. In this light, each piece of abstract art, no matter how abstract, is a legitimate part of an unfolding art narrative.

We are only able to respect abstract art if we accept that it is a legitimate part of the art narrative. A whole new world opens once we do this! Take a stroll through an art gallery with this new way of thinking. Ask the questions, "What is this artist trying to say? Who is she responding to? What does this make me think of?" Write down the different names associated with artistic movements. Look them up when you get home. Make a mental note about the movements that you preferred. Soon you may find yourself sharing your love for minimal realism and precisionism with your friends.

#8: Build Your Own Six Pack: Sample and Compare.
When finished, turn back to page 69.

To build your own six pack (also known as "Pick Six") is, in my humble opinion, the best way to purchase alcohol. You may have seen one of these "Pick Six" stations in a supermarket, a liquor store, or a gas station. Here is how they work: Distributors take a random assortment of beers, remove them from their boxes, and line them up in a designated section of the refrigerator. Then, the real fun begins. Customers are invited to take an empty cardboard beer carton. The six slots form a blank canvas. Scan the selection of beers and take a mental note of the beers that you have tried and the ones that you want to try. The entire experience is reminiscent of a childhood candy shop. You stand before jars of little gummy animals and sugary treats. With an iron grip you hold a small plastic bag that is ready to be filled and weighed. Allow yourself to get excited!

It's now time to make a decision. Here are a few strategies for choosing beers that I have developed over the years:

1. Same brewing company: Some suppliers will have multiple beers from the same brewing company available in the "Pick Six" section. Take one of each beer to sample rather than in-

vesting in a variety twelve-pack. This is an easy and cost-efficient way to form an opinion about an entire brewing company.

2. Same style: Pick six of the same style of beer. For example, try six different pale ales, stouts, lagers, etc. Compare the unique flavors that each brewery attempts to capture. Put the beers to the test: Which of them is the best? Which one will I avoid in the future?

3. Three and three: You and your friend each pick three beers without the input of the other. This strategy teaches us how others can help us get out of our comfort zones and try new styles of beer. Go home, sit on the porch, and split each one over a good conversation.

4. Mix and match: Throw caution to the wind! Pick any six beers that look good and call it a night.

I normally share the great responsibility of picking six with a friend. Splitting a "Pick Six" is the perfect way for two beer drinkers to develop a friendship of virtue and grow the community of appreciation. Find a friend who is willing to pay for half of the cost and drink half of the beer. You will each spend roughly $5 for enough beer to last an evening or two, depending on your limits. Set aside a time when you can sit and enjoy the tasting. Choose two similarly shaped glasses for easy splitting. Start by talking about the beers. Then, allow conversation to naturally flow to other topics.

A word of warning: Some stores will place their old, expired beers in the "Pick Six" section. They know that an unsuspecting "Pick Six" consumer is likely to purchase an expired beer by mistake. Take a close look at each beer before taking it home.

#9: Reflect on the Bread and Wine of the Eucharist.

When finished, turn back to page 72.

When finished, turn back to page 72.

Bread and wine are unique because they do not occur on their own in nature. There is no such thing as a bread tree or a wine bush; each product requires some degree of human interaction with the natural ingredients of grain, grapes, and yeast. Grain must be sown and milled; then it must interact with the right ingredients before it becomes bread. The words of the Eucharistic prayer reflect this sentiment: "for through your goodness we have received the bread we offer you: fruit of the earth and work of human hands, it will become for us the bread of life." Bread requires the "fruit of the earth," a gift from God, and the "work of human hands," our artistic participation.

Similarly, grapes must undergo a process of mashing, boiling, fermentation, and aging to become wine. The Eucharistic prayer again reflects this sentiment: "for through your goodness we have received the wine we offer you: fruit of the vine and work of human hands, it will become our spiritual drink." The Eucharistic wine requires the "fruit of the vine," a gift from God, and the "work of human hands," our artistic participation.

Bread and wine, therefore, are two perfect examples of the human calling to create. Humans artistically interact with the natural fruits of the earth, given to us from God, to create a gift that is appropriate to offer back to God. The Eucharistic elements embody the relationship between God and humanity, Creator and cocreators.

#10: Learn the Seasons of Beer.
When finished, turn back to page 80.

It would be an imprudent use of space to completely describe the seasons of beer in this book. Several texts — online and in print — have already done this in great detail. I encourage you to look up a book, blog, or website that provides a calendar for seasonal drinking. Simply google "drinking beer with the seasons" and click around. Try to memorize the details. Follow the calendar as close as possible to enjoy certain beers during their peak seasons. Compare seasonal beer to seasonal fruits and vegetables. Anyone who has had a peach in early summer compared to a peach in winter knows how much better they taste when they are in season. The entire experience is enhanced.

One idea, though, that is rarely discussed in these other sources is the virtue of prudence. Prudence, traditionally defined, means doing the right thing, for the right reason, at the right time. In our situation, prudence helps us discern when is the most appropriate time for a certain beer. It can begin with one simple decision: the beer we order.

Two major discernments occur when choosing a beer. First, the beer should fit the season. Second, the proper glass should be chosen to enhance the drinking experience.

First, create a quick list of criteria to use when discerning your beer choice. Some questions may include:

- What's the weather like? Is it hot or cold?
- What time of year is it?
- What is the occasion? Am I celebrating or am I having a casual beer with a friend?
- Am I pairing it with food?

As noted above, beer connoisseurs have created calendars that illustrate when certain beers should be enjoyed. These calendars are useful tools to help us become familiarized with the beers that we may see at a bar or liquor store. Yet, these calendars often fail to consider the occasions for which we gather and the purposes of our drinking. Celebrations often call for higher-quality beverages. Warm days often call for lighter beers. Think about the gathering you are about to attend and choose accordingly.

Congratulations, you have successfully discerned which beer is appropriate for your current situation! The next step is choosing the appropriate container for your beer. The glass is an important vehicle for enjoying a beer in its optimum state. Some breweries are aware of this and include a picture of the recommended glass somewhere on the label. Seek it out next time you have a craft beer in hand.

Many people think the glass doesn't matter. I thought the same thing until I compared drinking the same beer in two different glasses. For example, a pale ale has many floral notes that are easily missed when served in a mug or a pint glass. A tulip glass is shaped in a way that allows the consumer to swirl the beer and capture the complex smells and flavor notes. It is difficult to return to drinking pale ales from a pint glass after experiencing them from a snifter or a tulip glass. Even a wine glass is a worthy substitute in an emergency.

Some bars are stocked with the appropriate glasses for the beers that they have on tap. The bartenders are familiar with the benefits of each. This is a growing trend. But you might find yourself at home with a style of beer that you have never tasted. Luckily, your friends knew of your growing interest in beer and bought you a set of beer glasses for your birthday. The glasses lay before you: a snifter, a weitzen, a stange, a goblet, and the trusty pint glass. Which one will you try today?

It's not imperative that a consumer drink the appropriate beer at the appropriate season in the appropriate glass.

A bar will not rebuke you for ordering a Hefeweizen in winter. A good stout will not taste bad in a snifter. But recall from Chapter 2 that humans rarely settle for the bare minimum when a more fulfilling option is available. Not only can these small decisions make a good beer taste better, but being attentive to these small decisions can help change the entire way we look at life.

A seasonal beer drinker will eventually become a seasoned beer drinker. He'll take risks and try new beers. Some beers he'll avoid in the future. Others will be shared with friends. The ability to discern the appropriateness of certain beers grows as an individual learns to appreciate the many intricacies of beer. Prudence and artistic appreciation grow together.

#11: Give Your Prayer a Face. Make Prayer Personal.

When finished, turn back to page 112.

Think about the common phrase "put a face to a name." This is how we describe the experience of meeting someone after hearing his or her name used in conversation. The person is no longer an abstract idea represented by a word. He or she becomes a human being who fills our area of perception. In a similar way, Christians are called to "put a face to a prayer." We must put a face to the person in need of our prayer.

It's easy to remain distant from a subject when we give it a generic title. For example, we commonly pray for "an end to world hunger." It is easy to say this without making a commitment. Now, think about this prayer: "I pray that Roger can continue to find meal programs that are willing to provide nourishment for his entire family. I pray that he can continue to receive the food stamps necessary to put food on the table as he wrestles with a mental illness that restricts him from finding employment. I pray that the public transportation system is improved to give Roger access to a supermarket since he lives in a food desert." This prayer, on the other hand, requires commitment. We must truly know Roger to pray in this way.

Our prayers risk becoming selfish requests or comfortable platitudes if they do not have faces. Even though the sentiments "for world peace" or "an end to poverty and homelessness" are meaningful and come from a good place, they are not enough. They can be merely comfortable responses to a broken world and a burdened community of suffering persons. So we must become empathetic persons of prayer. We must join our brothers and sisters who suffer. Just as Pope Francis says that priests have to be "shepherds living with the smell of their sheep," all of us are encouraged to pray with the smell of those who are less fortunate than we are.[51] It is only possible to pray with a face if we are active participants in the struggle for justice.

So start by learning the name of someone in need of prayer. Bridge the gap between you and him and listen to his story. Then pray using his name. Try to avoid general phrases such as "those who are homeless" or "those who suffer from depression or anxiety." Use personal identifiers. By doing this, you will quickly learn how personal your prayer can become.

#12: Use Qualitative Language to Rate a Party.
When finished, turn back to page 115.

The party scene can teach us many things. One observation my friends have made is that Americans love to brag about how little they spend on alcohol compared to how much they drink. We boil down an entire drinking experience into *quantitative* expressions. Reflect upon your own experience of parties as I share with you a story to illustrate this reality.

In spring 2016, my friend Meaghan befriended at a coffee shop (and later dated) a man whose name was Falko. He was originally from Germany but was doing research and giving guest lectures in Ohio.

Falko attended many of our social gatherings during the length of his stay. It was common at these gatherings to share a glass (or two, or three) of wine. Our entire community flourished in the presence of Falko, who provided a fresh perspective on our American lifestyle.

After a few weeks, Falko felt comfortable enough with us to share an American quirk that he had observed during his visit. He found one thing peculiar (and somewhat comical) about the way Americans introduce a drink they have brought to share at a party.

One night, Falko picked up a bottle of wine at the local supermarket and brought it to my apartment to share. I said, "Oh, that looks good! I like the label." Falko responded, "Thanks, it was on sale and I got a great deal on it. It was only $4.55 marked down from $9.00! Perfect, right?" I thought nothing of the comment. Later, during a lull in the conversation, Falko asked for our attention. He apologized for using us as a social experiment, at which we looked at each other with quizzical expressions. He admitted he had been trying to "sound American" in his comments throughout the night and had passed his own test. None of us had noticed.

He observed that Americans are quick to share one simple detail about their recent purchases: the cost. Americans are obsessed with finding good deals and telling other people about them. It doesn't matter what the product is: clothing, alcohol, or furniture.

We all realized the quirk and shared a hearty laugh.

Our American tendency to quantify a drinking experience (counting our drinks, looking for the best deals on alcohol, or counting the ratio of men to women at a party) can distract us from the *quality* of an experience. Sometimes it is good to shut off our analytical, pragmatic minds and open ourselves to new experiences. Try this! Prepare for your next party by focusing less on quantitative measurements (the cost of drinks, number of cans in the fridge, or ABV of the drink in your hand) and more on the quality of the celebration. How will you evaluate this quality? I cannot say. But I *can* promise that your desire for pragmatism will decrease as you allow the spontaneity of the Spirit to increase!

#13: Consider the Nonverbals of Prayer.
When finished, turn back to page 128.

The most basic level of communication is nonverbal. These nonverbal cues include, but are not limited to, facial expression, hand gestures, eye contact, bodily posture, and physical distance from another person. Studies show that the vast majority of human dialogue is nonverbal.

Now, imagine having a conversation without any of these cues. Picture this scene: You are sitting back to back with a friend, expressionless and rigid. Only words are exchanged between the two of you. Emotion is only expressed through grammar and inflection. No matter how hard you try, only so much comes through.

This is an unlikely scenario. But consider popular forms of communication, especially email, text, and phone calls. Older generations dislike these forms of media for this very reason: It is very difficult to express ourselves and be understood by others if we cannot use nonverbals.

Our interest in the spiritual life makes us ask the question: What role do nonverbals play in our prayer? First, they are important for the community that is gathered. The *General Instruction of the Roman Missal* (the basic handbook for determining what is proper at Mass) encourages Christians to share a "common posture" during the celebration of the Eucharist (43). The liturgy is a communal movement of the Holy Spirit. We should move in solidarity with our brothers and sisters, whether we are standing, sitting, kneeling, or processing.

Second, the way we think about nonverbal communication is important. Consider how many Christians pray: Prayer tends to be more like texting than a face-to-face conversation. We send God a message and hope that it is read. Dialogue is indirect and nonverbals have little or no role. We keep our distance from God as we send our prayers to an impersonal Being. The type of faith that I have just described resembles the relationships among many young adults in our day. Time spent together, in person, has become a rare commodity. We have replaced face-to-face encounters with time alone on our phones. Communication takes place through screens.

Virtuous friendship cannot flourish in this setting. And, at its worst, it leads us to forget how to approach Christ, face to face, as a friend.

How can you, in the midst of this cultural reality, re-engage the physicality of your relationship with God and with others in your community?

#14: Compare the Catholic Mass to a Party.
When finished, turn back to page 129.

The parallels between a party and the Catholic Mass are

uncanny. Learning about their interconnectedness will help us better understand each one as a separate, but related, experience.

First, Catholics refer to Mass as the "*celebration* of the Eucharist." What's behind a name? Well, you may have heard some of the other names that are commonly used to define this occasion. They include, but are not limited to, an "assembly," "gathering," and "service." All these synonyms are influenced by the Protestant Reformation. The word used to describe the liturgy changed for Protestants as they altered the purposes and theologies of their respective liturgies.[52]

When we turn back to the Catholic Tradition, we see that none of these titles properly fit the true purpose of the Catholic Mass. According to the *Catechism of the Catholic Church*, the purpose of the Mass is to "celebrate the saving work of her divine Spouse in a sacred commemoration" (CCC 1163) and to "celebrate the mystery of salvation in the sacraments" (CCC 1139). The term "celebrate" has historical roots in Passover and the Feast of Unleavened Bread. Only the term "celebration" can properly reflect this historical and theological depth of the Sunday liturgy.

Second, the Catholic priest is called a celebrant rather than a presider or minister.[53] The title reveals his profound role. He guides the celebration, like a successful host of a party, by invitation, not by dictating commands. He must also strike a balance between two poles: structure (liturgical theology) and spontaneity (the Holy Spirit). The entire liturgy will be affected if he allows the congregation to adhere too closely to either pole. On the one hand, the liturgy risks lapsing into a bland sequence of movements and prayers if structure triumphs. Or, if spontaneity is not properly guided, the liturgy can explode into an irreverent orgy of self-exaltation.[54]

We can also see the role of the celebrant echoed in the host of a party. A good host works to ensure that the community shares the same goal: fulfillment. Some informal means of ensuring this goal include, but are not limited to

- inviting people who are prone to create an inclusive atmosphere;
- setting a playlist of songs to create a healthy vibe;
- controlling the music volume to allow conversation while discouraging immodest dancing;
- purchasing craft beer to encourage temperate consumption;
- avoiding drinking games that easily lapse into binge drinking; and
- determining a shared purpose for celebrating.

I challenge you to identify ways in which the Mass and a common party overlap. Start with the setting that you are more comfortable with and draw comparisons to the setting that you are less comfortable with. Both are, at the core, celebrations!

#15: Give Your Time, Talent, and Treasure.
When finished, turn back to page 133.

I struggled in my college years with the idea of almsgiving — giving a portion of my personal earnings to the Church. Why? Well, like many other students, I wasn't making any money!

I, like many Christians, believed that "giving" to the Church was confined to monetary offerings alone. My head hung each week as the usher walked past and offered the collection basket. I avoided eye contact and felt a pang of guilt. "Am I even giving anything to the Church?"

My campus ministers helped me find consolation. They encouraged me to think about the ways that Christians are invited to give during the forty days of Lent. I was reminded that we are invited to participate in three actions: prayer, fasting, and almsgiving. (We have already discussed prayer and fasting/feasting in Chapter 4. This segment will emphasize the third and final means of "giving," almsgiving.)

"But," I thought to myself, "this means that I can only 'give' two-thirds of what is being requested by the Church. Is this sufficient?"

My dad broke it down further. He told me the story of a time when our family, due to financial straits, could not give monetary gifts frequently. During these months he was reminded by a fellow parishioner that almsgiving itself has a threefold definition: We are invited to give alms in the forms of time, talent, and treasure.

Time: Time, as we discovered in Chapter 3, is one of the most valuable currencies. We can hoard it for ourselves, using it to progress intellectually or financially, or we can give it away. Sometimes a moment spent with a person in need is worth more than the world. A sheer minute of presence is priceless, and we are given hundreds of opportunities to share this gift each day.

Talent: Each one of us has been blessed with particular gifts, and we are invited to share them. The best way to thank God for a gift is to give it to God's people! Reflect upon what you are good at, and then give a personalized gift based on that talent. These gifts are often cherished more than any item that can be sold or purchased.

Treasure: This category is often what we think about when we hear the term "almsgiving." But treasure does not only mean giving money. It can refer to anything that is a treasure to us. Reflect upon what you treasure most, and practice the Ignatian practice of "detachment." Can you stomach giving it away? Who needs it more than I do?

I listened to the advice of both parties, my campus minister and my dad, and sought to fulfill each invitation in the setting in which I found myself. I was a poor college student with an eager heart, ready to give. My solution, believe it or not, happened to be the same gift that Jesus often gave: bread.

Prayer: As I kneaded the bread, I would reflect upon the day ahead and what meetings I would have. I held in my mind the individuals I knew I would encounter, saying a little prayer with each knuckle roll and bread turn.

Fasting: I would not eat any of the bread that I would bake for others. I would only partake in consumption if another person invited me to eat a piece with them.

Almsgiving — Time: I woke up an extra thirty minutes early each morning to activate, knead, rise, and bake the bread. Then, while I shared the bread, I intentionally asked questions about the other person. These conversations would rarely last under ten minutes, and they often took me away from the activity that I was engaged in (studying, working out, rock climbing, etc.).

Almsgiving — Talent: Many people do not have the time or energy to devote to learning the craft of bread-baking. Thankfully, my eldest brother inspired in me the desire to bake artisan breads. Now I enjoy sharing this skill with others who appreciate the smell, texture, and taste of real homemade bread.

Almsgiving — Treasure: I sacrificed my money to purchase the ingredients that I needed to make the bread (and the artisan butters that accompanied them). Although this seems like a small sacrifice, it was still a sizable portion of the small income I received from my campus job.

Spend some time thinking about ways in which you can give your time, talent, and treasure to others. All three are precious, but remember that all three were first given to you from God.

#16: Practice the Art of Toasting.
When finished, turn back to page 141.

The toast is a prayerful gesture. Toasts recognize humans in the same way that prayer recognizes God. It is a natural way to give praise and thanks.

There are two types of toasts: prepared and spontaneous. All of us are familiar with prepared toasts. We hear them each time we attend a wedding. They follow the meal prayer and often include many of the same elements. A good toast makes everyone laugh, tells a story, and is from the heart. A poorly executed toast is unprepared, causes awkward silences, or relies on inside jokes. Like many of the things we have discussed thus far, toasting is also an art.

I had a friend in college who would carry around a miniature journal in his pocket for occasions when he could toast in daily life. He would prepare toasts and keep them on hand. I asked him, "Why do you do this? Nobody toasts anymore." He responded, "The tradition of toasting others should be revived!" His comment made me stop and think. It made total sense! Toasting is a perfect reminder during a celebration to refocus our attention on people rather than the activity being carried out. Even a simple "Cheers!" or "To Luis, bless him forever!" brings the community back together.*

Two occasions are perfect for the inclusion of toasts: birthday parties and bachelor/bachelorette parties. Before a party, communicate the expectation to everyone who will be in attendance. Provide a simple prompt: "At some point in the evening, I encourage you to stand up and make a toast to the person being celebrated. Include a story, a joke, or a heartfelt comment about the person. It is as simple as

---

* My favorite toast is twofold and religious in nature. I exclaim, "To the Blessed Mother!" and everyone responds, "And her most chaste spouse!"

that!" It is incredible how powerful a gift a simple chain of toasts can be.

The second variety of toast is much less common but just as meaningful. The spontaneous outbursts of praise or the telling of stories can accompany the raising of a glass. We must rely on the Spirit to inspire such occasions. It isn't a coincidence that the inspiration of the Spirit goes hand in hand with the consumption of spirits. We must open ourselves, at the beginning of each night, to the inspiration of the Spirit.

Acknowledgments

The philosophy of this book was planted in my heart by my friends at Marquette University who taught me to appreciate the art of craft beer and the fulfilling role it can play in the season of celebration. There are too many of you to mention here, but you know who you are. Cheers!

Most of the content for this book developed out of lectures and conversations that I shared with students and faculty at the University of Dayton. I thank all of you who engaged me with a critical eye and a welcoming ear. I am especially grateful for the guidance of Dr. Kelly Johnson, my graduate thesis advisor.

Thank you, Ryan and Luis. We have shared enough "research" on friendship, beer, and celebration to fill volumes. I love you guys.

Everyone needs a good bartender. Thank you, Bill and Ryan, who always kept my coffee mug steaming and my beer glass full.

A special shout-out to Mike Ingram and Porter Lyons who were the first to read my manuscript and give me honest feedback.

Many of my stories come from family. Thank you to my parents, Doug and Catherine, and my brothers, Garrett, Austin, and Nolan, who taught me lessons that I never knew mattered so much. Also, thank you to my in-laws who have welcomed me lovingly into their traditions and family.

Most importantly, I thank my beautiful wife who has supported me through the writing and editing of this book. Our marriage has taught me more about friendship and celebration than I could learn in any book or lecture. I look forward to spending the rest of our lives celebrating the love we share ... over beers, of course!

Notes

1. A bock (also known as bockbier) is a strong and malty variety of lager that is usually consumed in the spring.

2. Alasdair MacIntyre, in his groundbreaking text *After Virtue: A Study in Moral Theology* (Notre Dame, IN: University of Notre Dame Press, 1984), defines this idea as a person's "narrative." He explains, "To adopt a stance on the virtues will be to adopt a stance on the narrative character of human life. Each human life will embody a story whose shape and form will depend upon what is counted as a harm and danger and upon how success and failure, progress and its opposite, are understood and evaluated" (p. 144). Our moral actions place us in a history of related moral actions, and we become another character in the tragedy. MacIntyre continues, "To enter into a practice is to enter into a relationship not only with its contemporary practitioners, but also with those who have preceded us in the practice" (p. 194). This relationship between ourselves and the other characters throughout history is a story or a narrative in which we have an important role.

3. Villanova University, "Focus on Alcohol Use and Protective Behaviors," *Prevention Points* 1, no. 2, accessed April 16, 2019, https://www1.villanova.edu/content

/villanova/studentlife/health/promotion/goto/resources
/archives/_jcr_content/pagecontent/download/file.res
/Prevention%20Points%20Alcohol%20Issue.pdf.

4. Please note: I intend to use "qualitative" both in a properly philosophical sense and also as a literary tool for your general understanding.

5. James Martin, S.J., Commencement Speech, Marquette University, 2014.

6. It is interesting to note that Aristotle uses the word "friend" to describe all three relationships when he could have chosen other words such as "connection" or "acquaintance." Maybe he was on to something. Think about the way college students talk about one another. We may refer to a classmate or a roommate as a friend by mere association. By the end of a night two strangers can be heard calling each other good friends. We hear the term "friend" tossed around with little thought. All of us are guilty of this, and Aristotle knows it.

7. Jean Vanier, *From Brokenness to Community* (Mahwah, NJ: Paulist Press, 1992), 44–45.

8. Ibid., 45.

9. I was blessed to hear this story as I shared a meal with Reverend Steve and Father Martin after they gave a talk about reconciliation at the University of Dayton.

10. Steve Stockman, "The Name," 4 Corners Festival, accessed April 16, 2019, http://4cornersfestival.com/the-name/.

11. Ibid.

12. Paul J. Wadell, *Friendship and the Moral Life* (Notre Dame, IN: University of Notre Dame Press, 1989), 123.

13. These are often labeled the cardinal virtues.

14. Thomas Aquinas, *Summa Theologiae*, II-II, 24, 2.

15. MacIntyre, *After Virtue*, 219.

16. Frances J. Connell, *The New Baltimore Catechism*, No. 3 (New York: Benzinger, 1941), 574.

17. Think about the way that the Church teaches about the Sacraments. A great deal of our time is spent learning about these capital "S" Sacraments. Very rarely do we hear about lowercase "s" sacraments. We must remember that, despite the importance of the capital "S" Sacraments, they do not contain the entirety of God's grace. We can learn a lot about God's grace by looking for the lowercase "s" sacraments.

18. Wadell, *Friendship and the Moral Life*, 98.

19. Thomas Merton, *The Silent Life* (New York: Farrar, Straus & Giroux, 1976), 27.

20. Aristotle, *Nicomachean Ethics*, trans. Richard McKeon (New York: Modern Library, 1947), 1165.

21. It is easy to understand why the strict policies on alcohol consumption have been created, due to various cases of abuse and lack of oversight. Regardless, much has

been lost in the process, and little effort has been made to make up for the absence of healthy role models.

22. Brewers Association, "Statistics: Number of Breweries," accessed April 16, 2019, https://www.brewersassociation.org /statistics/number-of-breweries/.

23. Mister Alcohol, "Super Bowl XLIX — Budweiser: 'Brewed the Hard Way' (2015)," YouTube video, 1:00, posted February 21, 2015, www.youtube.com /watch?v=gl_EdXSONOY.

24. William C. Mattison, *Introducing Moral Theology: True Happiness and the Virtues* (Grand Rapids, MI: Brazos Press, 2008), 119.

25. It's incorrect to assume that craft beer is never abused. It's also incorrect to assume that domestic beers are never drunk in moderation. Situations arise when each of these cases is true. But we must admit that these moments seem exceptional.

26. Pollan makes this argument in his book *The Omnivore's Dilemma: A Natural History of Four Meals* (London: Penguin, 2007).

27. Pope Francis, *Laudato Si* (Praise Be to You), 227.

28. Ed McCarthy and Mary Ewing-Mulligan, *Wine for Dummies*, 4th ed. (Hoboken, NJ: Wiley Publishing, 2006), 25.

29. Theological beer goggles, if you will.

30. G. K. Chesterton, *The Everlasting Man* (Garden City, NY: Image Books, 1955), 34.

31. International Commission on English in the Liturgy, *Christian Prayer* (Totowa, NJ: Catholic Book Publishing Corp.), 973.

32. Richard J. Foster, *Celebration of Discipline: The Path to Spiritual Growth* (San Francisco: HarperSanFrancisco, 1998), 20–21.

33. See "Sweet Baby Jesus: Exclaim the Name!," DuClaw Brewing Company, accessed June 18, 2019, https://duclaw.com/beers/sweet-baby-jesus-2/.

34. Marybell Avery, PhD3, Robert R. Rauner, MD, MPH1, Ryan W. Walters, MS2, and Teresa J. Wanser, MA3, "Evidence that Aerobic Fitness Is More Salient than Weight Status in Predicting Standardized Math and Reading Outcomes in Fourth- through Eighth-Grade Students," *The Journal of Pediatrics*, 163, no. 2 (August 2013): 344-348, https://www.jpeds.com/article /S0022-3476(13)00015-2/pdf.

35. The seasons can be considered one of the primary sources of beauty in the world, but that's a discussion for another day.

36. Pope Francis, *Amoris Laetitia* (The Joy of Love), 232.

37. Ibid.

38. Seeking the "top point of magnification" can be a dangerous game in which we walk a fine line between

tipsy and drunk, magnified and fuzzy. Although in the moment we may feel like we can keep on magnifying, more and more, we must ask ourselves if that extra drink will lead to the dullness of drunkenness as opposed to the steady magnification of merriment.

39. Hops are a common ingredient in the brewing process that add a distinctive bitterness and aroma. Hop farms look like vineyards since hops trellis on vines and grow as small green buds. Pale ales, India pale ales, and other beers with bitter notes are made by steeping hops early or late in the brewing process. Brewers are constantly experimenting with the variation caused by the endless combinations of hop species. The beers are also given distinctive hop flavors based on how early or late the hops are steeped in the beer.

40. Recall the friendships of pleasure from Chapter 1: Activities of pleasure can only be replaced by other, more fulfilling activities of pleasure.

41. Foster, *Celebration of Discipline*, 193.

42. Ibid.

43. Vanier, *From Brokenness to Community*, 46.

44. The entire Lenten experience can be transformed if we apply this logic. The extra money that we aren't spending on chocolate can be donated to a charity. The extra time that we would normally spend eating chocolate can be spent in prayer.

45. Saint Gregory Nazianzen, *Oratio*, 38.

46. Vanier, *From Brokenness to Community*, 47.

47. Some contemporary theologians accuse the disciples of drinking all the wine. Think about it: Jesus was probably not offered a "plus-one" but he brought his entire cohort anyway!

48. Robert Barron, *The Priority of Christ: Toward a Post-liberal Catholicism* (Grand Rapids, MI: Baker Academic, 2016), 76.

49. Ibid.

50. Annie Dillard, "The Writing Life," in *Three by Annie Dillard: The Writing Life, An American Childhood, Pilgrim at Tinker Creek* (New York: Harper Perennial, 2001), 597.

51. Pope Francis, "Chrism Mass Homily" (St. Peter's Basilica, March 28, 2013), *Catholic World Report*, March 28, 2013, https://www.catholicworldreport.com/2013/03/28/full-text-pope-francis-chrism-mass-homily/.

52. A name can say a lot about what a community believes. The way we name our celebrations will say a lot about how well we understand the need for feasting in our daily lives.

53. The latter two names developed in tandem with the Protestant naming of "assembly," "gathering," and "service."

54. Many theologians argue that our current emphasis on structure and rigidity is a response to the extreme, and sometimes troubling, spontaneity in the decades following Vatican II.